T0121025

An Epic Love Story

Princess Diana and her Private Eye
in Cincinnati

Spellbound – Unforgettable – Love Story

Private Eye

Rich

RICH MCDONOUGH

authorHOUSE®

AuthorHouse™
1663 Liberty Drive
Bloomington, IN 47403
www.authorhouse.com
Phone: 833-262-8899

Published by AuthorHouse 01/03/2023
ISBN: 978-1-6655-7932-2 (sc)
ISBN: 978-1-6655-7931-5 (e)

Library of Congress Control Number: 2022924105

Print information available on the last page.

This book is printed on acid-free paper.

"An Epic Love Story"

All the world must know how Proud Rich was in their times together. With Princess Diana's trust, belief, and love for Rich, is now telling all the rest of their adventurous 1993 love story.

"We both knew our Love Affair could only Happen Once"

"While working together now, but afterwards – never ever be with one another again. Because of who we were!"

If, Diana and Charles remained married, Diana was in line for Royalty, as the wife of the King of England, at that event

"There was no doubt, we would become 'derailed' because of the differences in our life styles and positions in life."

As well when you consider Rich, a middle-aged womanizer meeting his match with Princess Diana, it all becomes like 'Autumn in New York' a rare, precious, and fragile romance bloomed, that was forbidden and Can't Last".

Previously published book (2011):

In order to give the reader a better understanding of the current book being published for Autumn 2022, "I feel it would be important and helpful for readers that have not obtained the 1993 investigation book that was published by Authorhouse.com in April 5, 2011".

'To give further clarification, authenticity, and detail to the current upcoming 2022 publication.'

PREFACE

Princess Diana of Wales and Rich, a Private Eye - United in Working together to find Di's best friends Child, wrongfully taken to America, by the biological Father. A Known Drug King Pin connected with a dangerously infamous mid-western cartel.

Rich was called upon and hired by Princess Di, to search and find an eleven-year-old child taken from London. 'Di's childhood best friend's, child. Causing the mother to attempt suicide twice, worried she would never get her child back!

Princess Diana and Rich worked hand in hand together in finding the child. Many highspeed chases, dangerous confrontations and long-term surveillances 'while together', working out of specially equipped vans, with one-way glass.

"Not only were they successful finding and returning the child to the mother safely." "Di and Rich, became infatuated with each other, falling in Love, while in searching"!

Princess Di, had since gained a 'Loving caring Closeness to Rich'. As a result, in Di, loving, working and just being respectfully together with Rich continuously.

Princess Diana's Amazing, Extraordinary friendship between Di and her, Life Long, endearing relationship, through the years has now come to be tested of Di's peoples Loyalty she's known for.

Even though Di was legendary in giving of herself, for most really important matters. But this was not even enough in risking her life and position if needed, as she did. It all seemed like a bit much, too Rich. But Di was willing and wanted this to be done, at all costs.

And as well, possibly forgoing her life as the Princess, with the risk's involved to giving everything up to find this kidnapped child! Di, even sneaking out of the Royal Palace. Then secretly flying out of England, seemed remarkable too Rich for this friend. But Di's feelings were very, very strong as to the closeness between the two!

Hopefully, this was a truly reliable source, in this 'life and death situation, for Di's friend, in helping trying to recover the child, kidnapped over two years earlier by the biological father.

"In my opinion, Di, wanted to do it, 'because'– Di must know or knew who the child really was, but still keeping it all secret for some unknown reason. Hopefully one day it will all come out.

Her friend thinking the child would probably never be returned to her, and why Princess Di's horrifying fear of her friend killing herself, that was driving Di to do it. Di, dearly loved her friend.

This woman and the Bio-Dad had been living together for over ten years, and now separating. And the Bio-Dad lives at an unknown address in Cincinnati, Ohio USA.

The problem arises from the Bio-Dad. In all the years he had been living with her, they were never married. And he had been going through medical school in New York, in the USA, most all of that time and as well while living in London with her and the child, coming home to be with them when he was not in class.

On one of those periods at medical school, while he was gone for some time, she had met another man and wanting to get married to him. while the Bio-Dad was still gone, at medical college.

She was then in the process of marrying this man, when the Bio-Dad returned to her home in England. There of course was a lot of unhappiness over this, but the bio-dad finally got over it, and apparently tried to convince her, it was O.K.

And to be accepting. He offered to take the child back with him to America, while she was on her honeymoon, and then bringing the child back to her, afterwards …

She thought that was a nice gesture, so she allowed this. But when the Bio-Dad and his nine-Year-old child left, the child had never been seen or spoken to again.

later rumors surfaced that in the child's infancy, the baby was thought to have been female, 'but without certainty' and said to being reared by a doctor and his wife. Di, didn't know that.

Di's, thinking it was thought to have been the bio-dads child as he was that doctor then, with him, the Med student, then not a regular doctor. Her friend may have been the mother of that baby but not sure! Di knew that she did get pregnant right away after they started living together, and had another child soon after then – and since, Di and her, hadn't seen much of each other after the first child was born.

As well, somehow Rich got the impression this so-called life long and endearing female friend may have never lived with the bio-doc, very long, "but Princess Di maybe claiming that – to cover up her original thoughts, by claiming her endearing friend as that of the child's mother, 'who knows.' And for whatever reason-no one knew! It was somewhat confusing.

"Well, my job was to find and recover the child, the biological identity and so on, was not my assignment", but made me very curious as to why the search was so important.

"One of the main reasons, Di may have been so determined now' in finding the kidnapped child, - Risking it all now to find the child, as well to be sure in Di's mind!

"The bio-dad, purposely never left any address or phone number, and apparently, kept the child from making any kind of contact with the mother or Di."

Di's friend had never seen or spoken to the child since. She was said, to had gone ballistic, became an alcoholic went into rehab several times, and twice attempting to kill herself, over it.

not knowing for sure, but had 'Di' or her friend gave birth to the child and unmarried, never wanting anyone to know because of that, possibly?

"Di later pledged - total privacy and confidentiality to all, and especially to the Private Detective she hired to find the child"

'As well having him also pledge, but no actual mention as to the to the sex of the child, 'just that it was eleven years old now and when kidnapped about 9 at the time.

After Princess Di's Death, in 1997 Rich decided to write the upcoming book for publication. Scheduled to be on the street about November 2022.

Rich felt, he wanted the original readers along with the new ones, to know as much about the 1993 edition, along with the current book, to tell the readers what a great and wonderful person Princess Di was.

'As originally, Rich promised and pledged his confidentiality to Di, and for many years never disclosed much about the book or their love.

"Still, even though Di is gone, I will continue to keep most all facts, names, locations, dates, private.

CHAPTER ONE

━━━━━━━━━━━━━━ ⊂∞⊃ ━━━━━━━━━━━━━━

"Princess Diana of Wales: After relentless searching, and contacting, of higher ups in official investigative market resources, Di, did personally contact and hired Rich McDonough a Private Eye out of Cincinnati OH United States of America, to search, find and recover the kidnapped child taken from its home in London England, United Kingdom."

But to be clear, before this time, Princess Diana and Rich McDonough, the private Eye had never seen, known or met each other before. For any reason, either personally or for business".

Other than Rich having a possible sighting of Princess Di in the news, magazines or media, but unlikely.

'I mean, let's face it, Rich was basically a no body, so to speak, a lowly private eye by comparison, only hired for his expertise in that, to protect Di, her and the child in this effort, in dealing with the thugs in the drug Cartel.'

Had Di not called or made contact with Rich at his Shamus Detective Agency, they probably would have never met, yet.

But now – in Di, hiring Rich to work the kidnapping assignment together with Di, friend and the child's mom, helping Rich – "meant a 24-hour closeness for the two of them together – night and day, and Di accepting another role as just dating, on long term stake outs primarily with Rich, acting out as lovers for viewers".

But that was not known to Rich at first, Di requested she remained on the case 24hrs, a day being right with Rich, working-meaning accepting any and all contacts, flirtations with Rich acting as just a date to lessen their suspicion to police.

And for sure Di's confidant learned also that the Bio-Dad was without a doubt, a drug dealer, and somewhat of a king pin at that, since losing his medical license to make the product he was producing, that he stole from Princess Diana during their brief relationship.

Di was then given more info on the Bio-Dad through a second source, because the Bio-Dad was thought to be the owner and producer of a facility producing dietary formula supplement products, not approved by the government, not knowing the product contained harmful items.

with certain ones dangerous. As well he claimed also to enhance vitality, and survival endurance of life, if regularly taken.

Di, learned his product may also lead to certain types of cancer and or death-and the Bio-Dad uncaringly knew that, and was continuing on with it, when Di found out.

His company was said to have been ordered to withhold production, supposedly because there was no government approval for it in use, of a weight product.

He the Bio-Dad was attempting to use Princess Diana's name as a sponsor. Di claims the formula was originally an invention and or formula designed and thought up by officials of the Royal Palace, to help and enhance those in Royalty only.

And Princess Di, says the Bio-Dad wrongfully stole it. And Di, wants it back, and production to be denied. As it is medically unsafe. Di never ever backed him in having or producing it.

Bio-Dad outright stole the idea from Di. This originally was developed as an enhancement product for only those of the Royal Palace, of which Di, claimed and used.

This was another reason, that during the investigation to find and recover the child, that Princess Di, in working with Rich, was always, so 'imminent about going with Rich in each attempt to find the kid, which seriously put Di's life in danger in each try, because of the drug cartel protecting the bio-dad.

Later reports given to Di from her 'confidant in government regulatory position', that the wall between them, was being protected by sources to protect any interference between the

transporters and the drug cartel.

Di was also informed by her sources that the area in which the Bio-Dad was now guarding, had been extended quite extensively, and will have many more runners and protectors, of the product, causing even more dangers to the child's search.

Thus, now making Rich's job even harder, as we were now understaffed in that change…

For now, we decided to cease operations for the evening, and quit for now, we needed to eat and rest a bit, and Di was getting tired. So, we tried to wind down a little for the evening.

Di wanted to do a little window shopping and wanted to look into a few of the local women stores, for some additional thing.

Jer and the child's mom stayed on the stake out watching the Bio-Dad while he is in that gals apt. We noted the TV was on, at the house they were in, watching, so we told Jer to call me on the two way radio, if needed as Di and I were taking a little time off to relax a bit.

"We're nearby". Di looked around a little, and bought a cute mini skirt. Looked great on her, she already had brought heels with her, with her luggage. As well, she looked at some of the cheap costume jewelry, Di tried on a pair of big ring gypsy type rings, looked great on her. While we were there, she went in the dressing room, tried on the earrings and the skirt, 'short just 2" above the knees, she looked cute. With her new earrings, when she came out of the dressing room, slowly walking toward Rich, to see what he thought of it. Rich, said I just paid for the new things, you made good selections.

"Then she 'asked what did I think "I, said, I just paid for them-and you look great" as always, and so on.

Now heading out to eat!

The bar now alive, playing, and the singers and dancers were getting geared up for a good time, tonight.

'Di was talking to some of the people we had met there in the past as we were sitting down, and ordering things to drink.

Di liked the little fruit drinks with the umbrellas in them'. Almost as soon we sat down, men were rushing over to greet us, 'but really to see Di', as she was the pretty lady who danced with many of them in the past "and them hoping for another chance.

As we sat, an abundance of snacks and drinks brought over to us, "Di, then quickly pulled (Rich) up to the dance floor, hugging and caressing as we danced, having a great time".

A short time later were eating the most fantastic barbecue, enjoying all of our time, together. "Di, as always looked great, especially with her new skirt, and so on, dancing to the romantic music", in this well-known Louisville jazz bar.

"Di seemed to really enjoy it all, as she and I danced closely to almost all the romantic classics. Di without a doubt, was a woman that seemed to be somewhat starved for our closeness, in the attentive loving relationship, we both had for each other". "She told me all the time, how much she loved and needed our unique moments together!"

And after a long grueling day, not to long after, Di's telling me she was really tired, a 'long day' needing to get back to rest, as she is caressing my arm and pulling me to leave', . . . and we did, In need of some Rest!

A little later, Di was also informed that the Bio-Dad's area to watch over, had since been extended, and much more at risk in our involvement now Based on more information from one of Di's confidants.

Rich and Di, both will be taking serious chances and Risk's for Di's safety. Because of what else Di was told by her confidant, who had checked out the Bio-Dad through American intelligence sources, obtained through her friend in the Prime Minister's office.

Di, later told Rich, that the Bio-Dad, was now for sure, a drug dealer, since losing his medical license to practice medicine. Di was then given more factual information, through a second source.

And as well owning and operating a facility making dietary supplement products without government approval, used as a weight product, he had been manufacturing for a short time, and Di, very worried and concerned for the people that will be using that product, the main reason she wants it taken back.

Later reports given to Di, from her confidant, that since the X, had many thugs protecting him, who would not hesitate to kill if there was any type of interference 'such as us! While in pursuit of the child.

So, in Di and Rich's time together, working closely on the kidnapping, night and day, spending most all time basically side by side. As Di, had requested in their original agreement.

Di briefly commenting on the kidnapping, in saying she felt really bad that the young child, had been taken by the Bio-Dad, as the child was now just a young eleven year old.

Di feels that she had to alert authorities in the United Kingdom as to Bio-Dad's intentions. And all about the Bio-Dad's supplemental various kinds of illegal drugs.

As the Bio-Dad drove off each time, a chasing exposure for Rich and Di, was imminent, most of the times, doing highspeed chases - very cautiously, to where ever they took us too.

When not moving, doing surveillance when the Bio-Dad was stationery, with our stake out vans and so on, around the clock, in which Di and Rich were usually inside together watching them.

Because of the protection given to the Bio-Dad when he is transporting the product, he was being watched and followed by his own people, to be assured a safe passage in taking the product to the other dealers.

Rich knew this and had been confronted with similar situations and using extra caution.

Rich knew that the dudes following along with the Bio-Dad would be watching and looking out for law enforcement or whom ever, and take whatever measures needed to prevent them from being caught, apprehended or loosing product!

Then meaning Rich had to be on the watch for the spotters and keeping Di protected and away from unwanted threats of exposure by any of them.

"Rich tried to convince Di, of the serious nature in her exposing herself in any way, with the cartel's protection out there".

Still Di, seemed a little 'unconcerned' in that and wanted to go on as she has been, and "Rich not quite understanding her reason."

One particular protector-dude, had a reputation for hurting people, and linked to several hits and murders.

"So, we advised Di and, her friend to be watchful, and aware of that and others will be out there looking for any interference from anyone".

"Rich, still suggesting to Di, to let him and his team go after the Bio-Dad and take the risk needed, to find the child".

keeping you safe in doing what we have to, and hopefully we will be there, if or when needed.

Jer   Rich

CHAPTER TWO

———— ❧ ————

"To mention a really bad-incident, in which a main protector of product for the Cartel then believed out of the mid-western area, of Ohio had a hit to kill two area officers who had made a social buy acting as buyers using two young women, in their 20's and two young children. In the process of Cartel agents had been on them for a couple days, watching their partners, when thug's protectors went after the runners on the cartel.

After several shoot outs with them and - DEA enforcers the bust was eminent and both female actresses were killed, this was less than a year ago at the time.

I'm trying to impress the seriousness we have in making sure Di's safety isn't at risk, and it must be 'our number one priority".

Rich had to be somewhat emphatic with Di, about her safety. "Telling her these people involved in the drug business are not to be under estimated."

But of course, Di had led a very sheltered life style before then and usually her personal security and or body guards took most of all risk in any compromising situations – thus seriously preventing Di, from any exposure. And she was just - unaware and not to concerned of the possible dangerous situation she could be in, without her personal security she always had.

She seemed to be wanting to be more involved in the investigative things, not thinking about her own safety, but only catching the bio-dad.

"So, after letting Di know, she had to stay out of the game, and let Rich and his people do the chase surveillance. Di seemed concerned that I, Rich didn't want her to be with him, while chasing the dad in those high speed chases".

Rich 'hopefully' was thinking Di, won't go off doing anything, unless we knew. Yet Di had a need to know, where the dad was.

The cartel watching, was bad news, but Di seemed to be somewhat fearless. As I have said before, Di wants to help, and will take chances unless we stop her from taking them. And equally disregarding the dangerous cartel, her fear level was zero! She still seemed very determined to get the Bio-Dad!

"Of course, this is the reason why our surveillance was so important, both stationery and especially going from place to place", as the kid is most generally always with the Bio-Dad, and could be dropped off at any point of his travels.

"Where we had to know of, for the possibility of a recovery at one of those spots", us determining recovery attempts at each location, or where the boy may be left for a period long enough for us to grab the kid, and make a successful recovery.

"But if we're not behind them, we may miss the right opportunity-location, another reason for our 24 hour surveillance".

"But, should we not be on their tail most all the time, our recovery possibilities are dramatically hindered, and our attempts will be drawn out much longer".

Herein I'm submitting Rich's profile of experience, as we were originally asked for, explained Rich's life at this time –
somewhat, as to his experience, and performance abilities
needed in doing the investigative assignment, of finding and getting the kid safely from the captors.

Rich, was born October 19, 1938 in the city of Cincinnati Ohio USA and a lifelong resident, short of the three-time military tours, deployments to serve his country.

At the age of 15, he joined the U.S. Navy during the Vietnam era, spending close to a year, but then being honorably discharged, because the Navy learned he was underage, after a close buddy he joined up with was killed, and another lost a leg.

At age 17, he joined the Marine Corps Reserves for close to another year, serving out of Cincinnati, Ohio, on Gilbert Ave, U.S. Marine Fourth Signal co. As herein you could join at 17.

But this wasn't even good enough for him, he wanted to serve his country actively, so then joined the U.S. Air Force for another 4 years.

Training in telephone wire maintenance, and later performed investigative wire-tapping's plus, mostly in compromising areas. Lastly based out of Tripoli, in North Africa, before completing his final tour separating honorably on September 26, 1963

After all his military experiences were completed and concluded, he came back to Cincinnati and started his civilian career, attempting to stay in an investigative capacity, in all his future work endeavors.

Now a well trained former military man. Commencing and starting a civilian career as an insurance investigator, claims adjuster - investigator and later then became a bounty hunter, or better known as a Bail-Bond recovery agent.

Eventually starting his own Private Detective Agency, known as Shamus Agency, for the next 40 years plus, to date.

He became well known and highly regarded, locally, nationally and internationally to some extent for his effective ability to perform most all tasks. Then, gaining some substantial wealth thru earnings in those years, in those business connections.

His reputation, was considered as one of the best in the business. And at one time Rich even had a domestic case assignment of cheating on a U.S. supreme court justice, placing him under surveillance, whom Rich later busted for cheating.

The Justices mate was having an affair, and with another supreme court Justice! Rich was no doubt, one of the few with the ability to catch them, without being caught himself. His referral to this case given by governmental hi ups.

People knew of Rich's investigative ability with his covert connections, and his references that were all sent, to your lady confidant source working at the Prime Minister's office in the United Kingdom, per your request.

And of and through those cases sent to you, to contact Rich at Shamus Detective in Cincinnati, in the USA, for your needed help, on the kidnapping case.

"You called him and made an appointment to meet with Rich for that assignment and consultation upon your arrival in America".

Di, later called and made an appointment for the consultation as that of Princess Diana of Wales, setting up a one on one consultation.

CHAPTER THREE

BACKGROUND of Rich McDonough, professionally known as 'Mac' or Rich, and or just Shamus. Licensed 1972 in business 40 years. And herein an overview of his methods and activities of the day.

Here's a Short outline of 'Macs' career, indicating a couple of cases, he worked, that in no way, have any relevance or connection to the Princess Di. cases.

'Just a prelude' to reflect how Rich worked and to show the basis of Di's confidence in Rich's selection for her assignment.

Merely, noted just to show his ability and investigative style for your approval as to Di's choice in selecting Rich and the basic qualifications he developed and presented.

Along with this ULTIMATE 'Insiders look' at the Life of 'this' Private Eye, solving some of his most fascinating cases. In just relating for your knowledge. As to his uses, methods, and styles. 'Unlike most gumshoes', just to point out!

Mac had a real sense of caring and drive toward success, all through his career, with his relentless drive to get the true facts of the matter involved, and with having little concern for his own well fare, in moving toward completion and success on those cases.

If foregoing Dangers and risks were involved and a concern to get to the truth, putting himself on the front lines, was just a part of the job to get to that end.

"The following cases are just some of how 'Mac' worked his business. While the following are mainly some of his methods and reasonings used, they had no actual connections to "Princess Diana, and her Private Eye book now being published."

Mac, was his first name, generally used although short for McDonough, acquired basically while in the military. In there most everyone's was referred to as Rich or Mac. And it continued on thru his career.

The information contained in most reports, were not just given as bull, but facts as to investigative results.

But many times, the facts he developed were hard to swallow, but by the same token, usually hard or next to impossible to get or develop, from anyone but Rich, but he always seemed to deliver.

And costly to clients – and why most had to hire a detective, as getting that info usually was dangerous, time consuming and next to impossible to find or develop, generally.

Rich's experiences and abilities gained, were a result of over forty years, of real-life case histories actually worked by Rich.

While this in-fact Shamus was the name of his agency, it generally just meant, sleuth, investigator, detective and so on.

Since Shamus was the agency name, and a lot of people referred to him as just Rich or Mac, he felt it fitting to allow some clients and others refer to him as that of 'Mac Shamus' although, some didn't.

Rich

CHAPTER FOUR

In describing Rich's first office a little, (low budget) in those 'early days', and today, on an unusually early morning time of day for him to be there.

He had been on an all night stake out in one of Cincinnati's finest hotels, watching a cheating husband.

Since I, hadn't been at my office for over a week, I needed to make a check to see if 'it was still there' as Rich had many incidents with bad doer's, getting even for his success on those cases.

"It had been somewhat challenging, starting at the bottom, with little to no money, but I did".

I was fortunate enough to get this office free, in helping Jim Hartke a lawyer out a little on some of his law cases. The office had no gas, electric or water of which I had to get myself.

Jim was remodeling the building, and all six floors were vacant for now, as all tenants had moved out, because of the construction in progress.

Going to my office to do some snooping around and, getting the most recent messages off my answering machine, but hopefully to pick up some new cases, and or to see who else wants to kill me, as I deal with a lot of unhappy people.

And as well, maybe to pick up checks from paying clients on cheating cases, and as well, in listening to 'some clients complaining, . . . for their needed result's, I may have already found for them'.

At seven am, "really early for me, . . . usually sleeping in from all nighters".

While I stood_by my second-floor office door at 917 Main Street I could feel a lot of mail under my feet, as I was putting the key in the door - A great day so far, and downtown was full of hustling bustling people up and at them, already and probably eager to see and talk to me for results. And I guess I'm ready!

Then, I was somewhat blinded by the bright morning sun glaring through the frosted glass panel of my office door, projecting the sun rays to reflect the silhouetting door sign of "Shamus Private Detective Agency" all across the room and hall walls behind me.

As my office was on the second floor of an old six story brick factory building located in downtown Cincinnati, right in the heart of the busy business district, surrounded by law offices, county, city federal court houses, jails and such, 'that of an entire legal community, alive with exuberance along the city street markets and the daily hustling of eagers shoppers'.

The old fashioned eight-foot mahogany office door always squeaked loudly when opening or closing, as well it always slammed shut because of the updraft from the six floors of open and vacant offices about the stairwell leading up.

As I grabbed the door, I felt the pointed edge of a large brown envelope touching my hand, and I ripped off from its tape against the door, which 'someone' had taped to it, to make sure I saw, and got envelope. . . maybe a bill collector!

Looked like a subpoena at a quick glance, throwing it on to the desk along with a stack of mail and bills, over a week's worth.

And at that same moment, I had the shit scared out of me, by the sudden and loud, shrill cries and screams of two alley cats fighting on top of my desk - scattering papers and reports all over hell's half acres.

"My sudden presence must have scared the cats, who like to hole up in in this old office building, and as they were running across my desk top, each taking a three-foot leap upwards into a partial opening in the ceiling where a few ceiling tiles were missing and then scrambling out of sight!"

"The noise from the squeaking door as it closed, drowned out part of an incoming call on my answering machine".

"I faintly heard a woman's voice leaving a message. The only audible part I could hear then was her voice shuddering with anger and sobbing at the same time, with cries for my help".

The woman then crying loudly says 'Please call, call me, please ... right away ... my husband is with another woman, right this minute. I need to know if you caught them!

"There were six other callers, I had to listen to as well. And as this lady caller was hanging up, I could still hear echoes of her continuous sobbing, and pleas for help, before the line went dead, and was disconnected with the standard loud buzzing sounds".

This was a typical day of phone messages, mostly all cheating-domestic cases, 'but' what I did a lot of. That seems to be what we do most our investigation about, and I've been working out of this office over a year now, and doing well working these types of cases.

"Makes you wonder - if anyone is faithful" anymore, ... huh!

After recovering from the shock of the goddam cats and still a little out of it, from the early morning case. I sat down at my desk hopefully for a few restful moments.

"My next thoughts were for a cup of coffee, but after making a small pot and putting my feet on the desk, looking out on to the busy bustling streets, my phone started ringing off the hook, and probably with another crying woman wanting her husband checked out and watched."

"As I started sipping, my coffee watching all the pretty secretaries up and down the streets.

I took my first drink, sinking a couple of stale doughnuts in the hot cup of coffee to soften them up, enough to bite into for my breakfast."

"While I like the business, sorry to say - it's not the 9 to 5 delight, most like" – 'but this is what separates the 'real Private Eyes from the liar's and or bullshitters.

We're most always here, and ready to get to the real truth for our clients, if we can!

"I know a little over a year ago, I would have loved to have had the situation I have now, with being busy, making the bucks – but!"

CHAPTER FIVE

I'm ready for the big cases, and they are starting now.

"What a business".

"There is so much going on all the time' – "not now, even -thinking about the next forty years, of working all those cases."

"This is my place to be, I'm here and ready for it, my clients all seem to love what I do for them, and I get paid well, what else could a guy ask for?"

And one of those messages on my answering machine was a big-time lawyer

wants to pay me some big bucks, to get his client off an aggravated murder rap, and I, will be seeing him tomorrow for a nice retainer, and get started on that gig.

I have fixed my office part up, pretty good, and I'm happy here but the rest of the building is somewhat in serious need of rehab.'

Some of my lady clients, a little afraid coming in here!'

Jim and I have been in business sharing and happy, it's all working out. Jim's an attorney, gave me free rent in working for him part time on some of his cases.

Today attorney Ben Gibson, will be here to give me a big retainer on one of my first murder cases – from what others tell me, he is a big-time trial lawyers, and wants the cases worked his way, whatever it takes to get his man off!

"I can't get myself hooked up with a lawyer, who doesn't care if his clients are guilty or not – 'Yet … I do."

An attorney came in my office, but he can see if he pays a P.I. the right amount, the P.I. will make sure they get his client off.

"Not me, and I told him." While I'll work hard for you to get your man off, I will not lie or provide any 'creative' reporting'! that's just the way I operate!

So, if that is what you're thinking…forget it with me. I will never allow anyone to think "I'm your man."

The lawyer said he understood that, and didn't expect that of me, said just do your best and I'll make sure your happy, he gave me a nice retainer and I was off.

Not- if attorney clients really suspect their man did the crime, I'm getting the real shit (evidence) on him, one way or the other (Good or Bad) and that's that, I'm telling it, as I see it.

Most came into my office, throwing his business card on my table and said "you treat me right" and you will be on your way to the top, in this business!

After our long-drawn-out consultation and paying my fee, as he was leaving and saying, you being our man I can count on", and I then said "NO, that's not the way I work I'm nobody's man but I'll be there to do your job, and you can depend on that."

"I'm nobody's man", while I haven't been in the business a long time then, you'll be out of this office in a short while with the big money.

I said, "No - I'll do a good job, and you will know for sure if you have a loser with your client, but hear this, I'm nobody's man, I'll get the goods on him and that's what you will get, whether bad or good, and that's the way I work."

I'm not into that "Creative Reporting" and don't expect to be.

Then my phone started ringing, now another new client on the line for my help.

CHAPTER SIX

An attractive well to do lady, hired me to see what her husband is in to, and has been doing for the past few years.

She was one of these voices I got on my answering machine, last eve, says she thinks her husband is having an affair, and I want him just totally checked out, call me at this number don't leave your name or what this call is about, please

The lady client, said her name was unimportant and she was generally home most of the day and evening, "just say, you're returning my call, nothing else! And I'll get back with you."

Well, I called about nine thirty, after several rings, unanswered a female voice picked up saying 'I'm not available at this moment, would you please call me at your convenience, I have your number!'

Apparently, she didn't want them to leave a number that could be traced or checked out, as well saying maybe we could meet up for an interview sometime tomorrow, and hung up.

Eleven thirty, the client from earlier, was returning my call, saying, 'she would call me back in about ten minutes, her name was not given, so I waited.'

Close to midnight, this woman saying her name, returned my call, she talked very softly and educated, asking to meet for lunch tomorrow about one gives the location. So, I hung up and got ready to meet the next day.

Seven thirty am, the lady caller from last night, was on the phone and wanted to meet at one pm today at a lounge and I said "O.K".

About four hours later, the same lady called back and said, 'There have been a few changes, could you meet at my home about seven this evening?'

And gave me the address, only one of many of a high dollar homes in suburban Indian Hill area.

She said 'she will be alone, and her butler would meet me at the door, leave your car under the drive, thank you.'

After she gave me the address, I kinda, checked her out a little, in view of the address, learned it was the home of a heart surgeon, one of many in that area.

So in anticipation, I'm assuming this might have to do with a domestic situation, and probably a substantial fee could be on the line.

After I did a little more background work, knowing this doctor has a reputation as a player, I headed to the meet.

The home here had a long drive wrap around to the door way I would say probably a multimillion-dollar home.

After parking my car, the door man let me in and took me to what I would call a parlor where I was alone.

About five minutes, I saw a long pair of beautiful legs in high heels, slowly coming down from a spiral staircase. A lady of about 42, 43.

Dressed in a sexy black evening dress, 'her gazing over toward where I was, checking me out, I suppose to see what I looked like.'

As the lady was now down, she slowly turned and started walking toward where I was waiting.

I could see she seemed to be an attractive lady, long wavy brunet with a very engaging smile, well made up. Hanging diamond ear rings, and lots of diamond wedding rings.

I watched as she continued to slowly walk, noticing purposeful hip motions, very graceful as she got closer and then putting her hand out at me to shake hands, as she said "Hello, I'm the woman whom you spoke with."

Thinking to myself, WOW. I then said "I'm Rich, and they call me Mac. And very glad to meet you, ma'am."

She had one soft, but sexy voice as she told me what she wanted.

'I have been married for over 12 years, to the same man who is a physician, and heart specialist. We have no children; due to a medical problem my husband has.

He is gone frequently out of town and working when not traveling.'

'He of course is handsome man of 38 and he is always gone'.

'I'm thinking he just doesn't want to spend much time with me, for some unknown reason, and as you can see, I think I'm still somewhat of an attractive woman of 41. And I'm not quite sure of my suspicions as to why it is, that he doesn't seem to want to make love to me, and if he does it's on a very limited scale.'

'As things have been like they are now for over three years, I'm thinking I don't even love him any longer as a result, but when I confront him with all my suspicions, he refuses to talk about it, and heads out.'

'I'm suspicious of several of the pretty women he works with, but not sure if that's what the problem is.

My father is a very wealthy man, and he actually paid his way through all the best schools and colleges and is responsible for him being a highly regarded heart and brain surgeon and general physician.'

'My husband, is only 39, never married before, and as well I think he may be 'Gay' although I'm not sure, as he has numerous male friends, and physician.'

'He travels a lot, and spends a lot of time in the Jamaican islands and other closely related ones, and is really into

"supernatural activities and healings." And that really scares me a lot.'

'He is very concerned with his personal manhood, "if you know what I'm talking about," such as sexual abilities, manhood, erections and so on. And one time 'inferred that several times a year he goes to Vudu places and such, to be "re-generated" with the special rituals and animal bloods, that he really uses. "He thinks ... keeps him going.'

'I'm really afraid now, as in the past year he has been in the Vudu vicinity in New Orleans and other places. Talking with practicing "Medicine men", not real physicians and he even has a friend, he calls her, who also is in to that and who goes with him, and I feel they are lovers.'

'I have a lot of things to tell you, with a lot of proof I've been putting away, if and or when something really goes down and I need someone with your ability and to get involved and help me, "as I want out of this marriage".'

'I have been a good honest woman, and have not cheated on him for any reason, but I want a normal life, and with a real man who cares for me.'

'Can and will you help me? I'm not worried about cost, my dad already knows about all of what I'm telling you, and is ready to help me as well.'

'I'm a little worried because my dad paid for everything in her husband's life, of which her husband has never offered to repay him anything.'

'He is making wonderful money now, but has never once offered to give my dad or me back anything, and I think he is planning on setting up a medical facility with Vudu type medicines to aid in men's future.'

'My husband is very handsome but very unusual with his personality, almost like sometimes he is on cloud nine or something, and I'm afraid of him at times, another reason I need and want you to look into all of this.'

'I'll pay you well and all your expenses. And above all, I especially need your pledge of total confidentiality, as if any of this gets back to him, I don't know what he might do.'

'So, let's meet tomorrow about eleven, I'll give you the retainer, and photos that I have, and other instructions. I'll be giving you $5,000 in cash, so there is no way to trace it back to me, is that O.K.?'

'Start As soon as you can, what other additional you'll need for all travel expenses, let me know tomorrow.'

'I of course will be assisting you with everything you need, and I'll be there for you in your travels and so on to get the proof and or evidence, I need'.

As well, her husband is involved in several different drugs he uses constantly, and got involved with them while in med school.

'This one particularly lovely woman of 28, is a provider and heavy user in the drugs and the whole situation.'

'She lives here in Indian Hill in a large home nearby, with her "husband who in fact is a retired pharmacist", but I'm not sure if he is in on all this or not. Or for that matter, don't even know if he is suspicious of his wife and associate, or not. Another thing I need to know soon as you can find out.'

'I do know, he goes into the jungle somewhere around Kingston, for days at a time. I tried to follow him down there, but stopped my surveillance near the boat dock, as it is just too dangerous, I could see right away. So good luck and be careful.'

'Be talking to you in the morning at our meet, I hope!'

'By the way should you want or need my assistance there, or anywhere else I will make myself readily available, upon your call.'

'By the way, I forgot to tell you, that I went with him on a medical convention held near New Orleans, and it was very plane for this kind gathering of activity and of course covering various Vudu situations of which he is very much into.'

'One of the evenings after he and I had dinner at one of the French restaurants that are really big on Vudu things, he got a long distance call on his cell, but couldn't hear because of the glaring loud music, and gave me the motion that he had to go to some other part of the facility where we were to hear better, he was gone well over an hour or more.'

'I finally went to see what was going on, but couldn't find him anywhere. I asked one of the servers, and he said "Oh yes mam" - he and his wife, just left in her car!'

'Humm, he was gone for over two hours, and when he came back, claimed he went with another doctor on some business.'

'He wasn't aware what the server had told me, and I didn't let him know what the server told me, then.'

'I think he went to one of those Vudu conventions being held nearby, but he wouldn't say anything else about it.'

'I later asked him who the woman was! At first, he said "What woman?"- sort of denying it at first, until I confronted him that the server told me you left with your wife, then he started getting nervous and said "that was the doctor" he was supposed to see while there! He then said he never wanted to tell you it was a woman. Because of your jealousy.'

"The server said she was a pretty lady about 30, in a long red gown, now you're telling me she was a doctor? So, these are of the things I need to know about, right away." I told her, "As soon as we can put a few things together along with some other facts I'll be back to with you."

"As far as the New Orleans gig, you need to tell me what hotel you both stayed at and whether or not you had a car there of your own, or just a rental."

"In the mean time I'll be running a sheet on some the people you have mentioned, to try and develop a little info."

CHAPTER SEVEN

And now to 'Re-iterate' the original publishing basis of my 1993 book –
of which then was titled: 'Cincinnati Private Eye Protecting Princess Di.'

Should you not have a copy the 1993 book, go to your local public
library or get a copy of it on line.

Now, the Re-telling of those pages from the "Selected incidents",
and as well, about our Love Affair, I choose from the 1993 book, to now
be included in this upcoming version 2022, that hadn't ever been told
involving the most dangerous incidents, in finding and recovering the
kidnapped child.

After Di's returning to England, Di and Rich, never ever saw or had
any more contact again, with Rich as we both already knew we wouldn't,
get that chance.

Since Princess Di was killed in 1997, even though they,' Rich and Di,'
hadn't been together since 93, when Di, went back to the UK! After the
kidnapping investigation of getting the child back with his mother was
completed. In view of Princess Di's death, Rich really 'felt lost' again,
considering his deceased wife, Ethel's long time passing in 1982 before that
fact Di had passed, also brought a definite loss in thinking about Ethel.

And now Rich is alone again, in memory of losing both loves of his
life, in their tragic deaths.

And now Rich is again leaning more toward belief in the reincarnation
of Ethel and Di, back in 1993. Because of all the coincidences back in 93
and even now in 2022 for Rich.

As both loves were spontaneous' and at 'first sight', dramatic, climatic
and exciting, and both instances became priorities' - in Rich's life
immediately, then in those times.

Also — we are now explaining to the world, about the Love Affair between Rich and Di, in 1993 as to the significance, in why and how it all happened, In Rich's words.

In covering reasons, for their 'LOVE AT FIRST SIGHT' thinking phenomenal fact. While it may seem to be viewed as a questionable event, for some people as to the credibility.

In this case, it happened when he (Rich) was first introduced to Di, back then in 93. at the time of their first meeting-consultation about the kidnapping assignment' as Di was relating it to Rich at that time. "Rich's original involvement in this book, was of course my being hired to find the kidnapped child for Di "of which we later, were successful in finding and getting the child back to his mother safely.

I, did then tell the world, after Di's death in 1997, of our Love and relationship. Which did take place in 93. When Princess Di and I, did in fact fall in love. Primarily due to the long periods of time working and spending together in that dangerous risky situation, that brought us even closer together, worrying about one another in searching for the kidnapped child. The bio-dad was a nut, and would be dangerous.

This further 2022 publication is basically told as to the details of that kidnapping surveillance investigation, of which we did write, but Di, not wanting to tell the entire story in that publication then, at Di's request then.

The book written in about 1993 was not published for two years. Because of Di, much insistence to not tell the entire incident of the dangerous times, were left out then, along with some other details, now included in 2022.

And in my opinion as to how and why our love did happen, was not just because of Di's beauty or "love at first sight"- but to defend my thoughts, related in this book, was the possible reasoning in my belief — possibly because, of the coincidence and or suspected reincarnation of my late wife Ethel, that may have brought on this questionable event.

But as well the dangerous events occurring later in that book, brought us even closer, and I have, included prematurely in first part of this 2022 book, by passing other parts of the first book.

Here in, I'm now relating to one of the most dangerous incidents Di, and I encountered in conducting surveillance of the Bio-dad, with highspeed car chases, various confrontations and very long enduring hours, then in the Cincinnati areas.

But now, as well - in Maricopa Arizona, in a Near death experience for Di. I have included in the earlier portion of this new issue, relating to the serious incident for us.

And with this continuous risk, in worrying about what the druggies would do to us, if caught while we were chasing them.

Or if the bio-dad in being a king pin in a mid-western drug cartel, he controlled operations, dealing and negotiating deals, and buys. What do you suppose he would have to do to Di and myself, had we been caught? Especially with him knowing who Di and I were and why, as to the reason we were after him now.

Late one evening after being out all day doing surveillance mostly on the bio-dad and child finally. As he went back to the Loft apartment where he was staying. And a little while after getting back, we overheard him talking on his room intercom, of which Rich had already re-wired to listen in on, from room to room, to set up a buy. But out of town. The caller apparently calling from out of the area, was trying to set up the buy.

Turned, out to be out in Arizona, near the town of Maricopa just near Phoenix somewhere.

After a pretty long conversation, made arrangements for the bio-dad to fly out and meet up with them there. Had a big buy, and planned to hook up tomorrow afternoon at a private home in the Maricopa vicinity, near US route 10, about one to two pm. Dad telling them, he probably would have his eleven year kid with him, so at least now, we knew the kid was going then.

They made arrangements for the bio-dad to check in the Royal Palms motel, or something -couldn't hear then, due to static on our intercom. The deal was confirmed,

I, immediately made plans for our agent to set up our plane for the trip, and to be here at the loft Apartment's early, tomorrow to pick up myself, Di, and her friend.

In the mean-time planning to be watching the hotel here for the bio-dad's arrival to see if the kid is with him.

After our plane's arrival, here at the hotel and we see if the kid is here with him, and then we wait to see if the child goes along, or If he leaves the kid here, and if he does, then after the bio-dad leaves for the meet, we will grab the child and be gone. If he in fact doesn't go with him to the meeting.

Our pilot arrived here at the Loft and ready to go once we see if the kids stay here or not, or if he takes him, so then we headed out for Arizona right away in anticipation of their arrival.

We got to the soft landing field, near Maricopa, we arranged for. Why our plan to be here, so if in case were seen in doing the pickup we wouldn't be encountered by law enforcement if we got the child, that is if the kid goes on the trip with him.

If he leaves the kid, here at the hotel in Maracopa we will just grab the child and fly out to Cincinnati, right from here.

The bio-dad arrived in Arizona, and came to the hotel where we were already waiting for the bio dad. We didn't see the kid, although he could still be in their car, and once they drove off to the meet we of course chased after them, but keeping a distance from, as not to be observed, since we couldn't see the kid in their car.

Our agent back at the hotel will look around for the kid, and call us if he is back there and we will just grab the kid and wait for 'Rich to return, here to the hotel'.

'Still no word from Rich as to seeing the kid, in the bio-dads car so the kid must be in their car, sitting low in the seat or asleep'.

He started slowing down, in a somewhat desolate looking area with only a few ranch type houses and barns, and a lot of sandy desert, with plenty of tumbleweeds strolling about in the area.

There was one residence just down from the one for the meeting, as he slowed down to pull into that driveway.

Rich had to start looking for a stake out spot, but not on the side of the highway, they would see us and maybe cause some problems, maybe thinking we were cops.

Rich did see an old deserted structure about a city block away, from the meeting, situated on a sandy vacant lot, and then pulled in, without them watching.

The place here where Rich stopped was an old abandoned and dilapidated Mexican type Cantina, with faded pink paint, which was about a one and half story. Sitting pretty far off the road but close to the edge of a cliff. With one rear side of it hanging almost, over the edge. This was about we could find and so

we decided to stake out here, as there are no other places. The upper level of the cantina may give a better view of the area of the meeting, and maybe seeing better, if the child is here.

There were two old café type doors, hanging, but one almost of, and a couple of wooden steps at the entrance, door.

Most of the windows broken out. 'This Cantina was definitely what we thought was a life saver, we thought' at first, But later maybe death trap!

We saw the bio-dad pull in the driveway of that house, there was several other vehicles also in the drive. Because of all the wide open spaces, it was a very hard to stake out, because if the subject tried and wanted to, they could see about anywhere, around.

This at first seemed to be a perfect place for us, we thought. The lot where the Cantina was situated, was basically just all sand and tumbleweed everywhere…

As we described earlier, it was a great location for us watching, but as we kinda strolled around the property a bit, the other side was doomed. As it hung somewhat over the edge of the cliff, where there was about a thousand foot drop off into the Gila River valley, ravine below. Covered with rock and boulders, all the way down to the water, rushing below. Somewhat of a beautiful view, but really dangerous.

As I said, a beautiful site, but a not so good a place to live or be around for long.

Anyway, the area was continuously sand blowing, along with a lot of tumbleweed and such, making it somewhat hard to see and breath, as well.

Every now and then, gusty winds and so on, we noted when the winds blew, causing parts of the Cantina to shake and move about.

So far, the bio-dad is standing outside his vehicle, with papers and so on lying on the trunk, as he and others were peering over them as they talked. Rich said it looked like road maps they were looking at.

And then Princess Di, yelled to Rich that she had to find a toilet or something, as she was very uncomfortable and started searching around to relieve herself.

Thus, going into the Cantina searching for an appropriate spot for what she was going to do her thing. But most of the area was open and in clear view of the others about, no one here...

As Di walked around searching a little, things inside the cantina were falling and breaking as the wind kept blowing. Finally, she decided to go up a short flight of old wooden steps to the upper level, for a better place to do it...

All the time, the wind and sand blowing all about, making it hard to walk see and hear, a bit concerning because of all the crackling, scraping and parts of the building moving and sounding as it was falling apart. But it's been doing this for some time now, as it's been here long time, withstanding it – figuring it must be O.K.

Finally, Di stopped talking, apparently, finding a spot. And just as she was finishing, several high gusty winds started blowing, ravaging part of the structure near where Di was, and part of the walls and fixtures started coming loose and falling near her.

She started getting worried, and asked if Rich could come and get her. As she had become blocked on that upper level where structural beams and boards had fallen in the side that Di was. One beam fell down and against her leg and foot, and she couldn't get down or move, because of it, then yelling to Rich for 'Help.' The boards didn't hurt, but just pinned her down and unable to move about much.

Rich was on the far side, trying get to Di, but he too suddenly was somewhat pinned in where he was, so Di was stuck and couldn't free herself, and sort of crying while calling Rich.

At this point both of them were unable to free themselves, but after another strong gust of wind, blew parts of the area where Rich was, he freed himself and now trying to get to Di.

The rest of the steps leading to that area of the upper level where now gone, leaving no way to get to that upper level.

The last gust of wind blew so hard, a part of one side of the roof collapsed and fell into the cantina, Di, said she felt the building sort of sliding toward the back of the canyon, and her trying to get out- but couldn't, she now was at one end of the upper level, and could see no steps or other way, still calling out to Rich, as he continually responded asking her where she was and so on.

Suddenly a partition or wall fell, clearing Rich's sight toward the area where Di's voice was coming from and finally saw seen her on the ground there.

He couldn't go toward her, as he was blocked, and suddenly fell or knocked out from the side, and on to the ground.

After Rich was up, he called to Di again, and she told Rich she was then by the other far side, but still on the upper level with no steps or ways to climb down.

The Cantina then started slowly sliding toward the end of the cliff, then Rich told Di to "Move all the way over toward the parking lot area", and she did. And at that time Rich could see her on the upper level, and he decided to walk toward that area on several large beams or planks, that were not secured very well, as he stood on them. They bounced up and down and were swaying back and forth, side to side.

Rich got on the two boards and started walking slowly, again toward Di, still unstable in bouncing – Rich called to Di, and told her to "Move as close to the wall where the two windows below were." As they both were trying to get to each other, suddenly the far side broke loose from being connected or secured to the main structure crashing and fallen down the to the ravine and toward the water below.

Rich now closer to the wind yelling to Di, "to kick or somehow break the panes in those two windows, and when you do, slide down and stick your feet and legs out, as far as you can".

As Rich was moving up closer to the windows and grabbing onto her feet, legs and thighs she was working her way down and out of that window. Suddenly Rich grabbed her hips, pulling her down and out into his arms

And at just about that same time, high winds simultaneously started pushing both of them, causing of them to fall backwards into the sandy parking area.

Now, safely far enough away, as stormy high winds blew the two of them farther and even more out of the way for some reason - which prevented both of them from being severely injured or killed!

Now when portions of that side of the Cantina started falling, toward where they were and preventing, the heavy debris from falling or hitting them.

The two them were far from the main part of the Cantina now, as they held each other, caressing like that could have been the last time – for them – and it almost was!

Further explanation of the situation while they sort of are recovering from that "near death incident", relaxing side by side, still having a hard time letting, go of one another.

Humm - those simultaneous winds, blowing the both them out of the way of the falling debris a lucky, "once in a lifetime" occurrence and is known as the very same thing. We had once before in Di's first meeting with Rich another COINCIDENCE.

But the world knows of Diana's deeds and legendary life. I have to say, they all should be even more proud now, her risking her life on this case "Di was just a continuing Hero" - in my eyes, and the rest of the worlds!

And we watched, the rest of that Cantina on that side, fall down, at what looked like to have maybe been over a thousand foot drop to the water and rocks below, Di, got out just in time.

As we talked and thinking, about that incident- "Why Now?"

For as long as that old Cantina had been there, and in that bad of shape, for so long time but still just sitting in that spot all this time. Makes you wonder – Why did it fall now?

Maybe another coincidence to show how much we really needed each other – "I don't know," but luckily, they both are still alive. Happy and in Love, even more!

In our 1993 book, this incident was noted, but not to this extent then, as to that dangerous incident indicated in the new issue of 2022. that was kind of played down by Di's wishes back then.

But now since Di's passing, we tried to tell it all, and at the time Rich was introduced to Princess Di. Rich was just flabbergasted in seeing this woman saying she was Di, as her resemblance to Rich's late wife, was remarkable. In view that this, lifesaving incident just now, may be part of the Di and Ethels paranormal

Was this just a coincidence now or what? Rich thinking maybe a part of that suspected reincarnation, thought.

The fact is - No One knows! But Rich, was still very happy in thinking of it, as "Ethel and Di's" demeanor, personality and overall appearance gave some credence to the happenings!

Rich thinking, maybe luck, or another phenomenal coincidence as to the two women. Maybe because of who Princess Di is in some kind of paranormal intervention.

During their initial meeting when Di, was touching Rich's fore arm, in sort of greeting him, substituting as a hand shake!

Which was one of Rich's wife's similarities in meeting a person, added another "paranormal" thought.

But since I'm directly involved stating my personal opinions in this book, about this particular aspect, that the readers will rely on their personal view as to the reality of my feelings.

I'm not inferring to my actual believability in my statements being true or not as to the other supernatural possibilities.

But at Rich's first sighting with Di, - even then, Rich already knew! And had that feeling, just being with her, and not only because of her beauty or even who Di's was!

But, because of the uncanny similarity and likeness to his first wife Ethel, he (Rich) was immediately attracted with exuberance in his sudden connection with Di.

But of course, unbelievable-momentarily, then Rich, regained what he thought may be happening, and thrilled to death in the possibility of some type of reincarnation or just a coincidence, with this sudden connection... And Rich Loving every instant of the event, even, if Rich was just "Day Dreaming" or plain out wrong!

But, believe me, it really does happen," More often than Not"

As-well, just to show the 'LOVE AT FIRST SIGHT' between Rich and Ethel, Rich's first wife. . . is also summarized herein, to prove a point. "As both situations were just meant to be".

Hopefully readers may gain some real in-sight as to this "Rare-but very likely" phenomenon that has played a significant part In Rich' life. And reflecting in a good portion of this book.

"Love at First Sight", Does it, or will It, happen more than once? "Yes"

And - IT "HAPPENED TWICE" With me, (Rich's) further EXPLAINATION and opinion about why Rich was fortunate enough for that to have happened twice.

Then of course, why Di, secretly snuck into America to help Rich find the kid. In the 1993 early book version. Di – secretly slipping into America without telling anyone in the Royal Palace or family, because she knew the Palace security would not let her and friend go, and Di, feared, telling them would put her help for her friend in jeopardy, so she didn't tell anyone!

To clarify in my opinion a few other aspects of that 1993 book, such as explain to the readers why Rich always seemed to be close or near to Di most of the time, was because #1, Rich was her body guard and protector then while officially on her kidnapping case, as she (Di) made and wanted that agreement originally.

Di took more chances than she should have, just being out and about. But actually, Di had unknown and personal reasons, "as well" that none of us understood, then.

Most assumed Rich was quickly attracted to Di and fell in Love, right at that moment, but later in this book – Di tells of that secret reason for the closeness to Rich, being out with him each time he went out to work.

But later in this book, Di tells of that secret reason for the closeness to Rich. Di, later admitted she withheld from Rich, the truth as to how long she and the Bio-Dad dated, and Di was ashamed to admit she dated him longer, allowing him in gaining more things about herself (Di) then he should have.

Seems Di told the Bio-Dad about a somewhat secret health issue or ideas for a useful product to be made to help women of the Royal Palace stay slim and look good through control of their weight, skin and complexion, and so on.

Di, of which never got her copy of those formula's back from him, as she never sat down with Bio-Dad long enough for him to make copies for her, so she could write them down.

And this then, was why she (Di) was always taking chances going out alone to check some things out, as to whether or not Bio-Dad was actually trying to duplicate the formula of what she told him about. He the bio-dad once told Di, he would like to commercially produce the formula's Di, told him about, thus using Di's name as advocate of the product. And she didn't want that. And insisted that he return everything he took.

Di, never really got the written documents and or formulas that he took from her. And I, Rich asked her about that, and she told me some of it, and I wrote it down as she told me, to the best of my ability. Never getting all of it. I wrote things down.

But not sure of the exact spellings for some of the things. Below are some of the items, I could best recall and unsure of the actual spellings and so on. But just for the record here was some of it below, best I could remember.

King Hyderotherapy Advocate for Colon Cleansing

Colonics & Hydrotherapy Mirodi formula

Claims additive claiming could revitalize and add years   to life, in the formula he was trying to put together along with his special medications and drugs he had to access to it.

Medical Safety Standard in England and the U.K, Di told Rich did not ever give approval of their government.

Di wanted to get the information to them, to see if Bio-Dad had been doing any productions of that, of which he intended in inferring Princess Di, was an advocate or something.

Princess Di, does not want to be any part of it, and told him so, numerous times, and reasons she goes out with Rich each time.

Di took my hand written notes, and Rich was going to make a better list, and put other items from some more of her notes with it, to give to the authorities. Di said 'He told her of many ideas he had for the production of the product. In him making some kind of supplement product he would actually put some kind of drugs in.'

Because of who Di was, along with her beauty, just about any one, would want to be with her and get in on the product she was supposed to have sponsored, and backed. The bio-dad continued to tell Di, how rich they both would get in this.

We have decided to stop working for now, surveilling the bio dad later.

Again, it was getting late, usually Di and I sort of shut down in our work effort about 10 to 11PM, and have again. We went for a walk, looked around in various boutiques, Di loved to just go in and look, and do her day dreaming trying out clothes, jewelry and "want nots."

We walked around, Di trying on different garments and so on, and her always kidding me with various things, she would always ask me what I thought of them, and kiddingly, we would talk about each.

At times, she would get carried away with thoughts, and sometimes just grabbing me with a quick lip lock – but finally let go, with a tremendous long hug, and usually saying something- I, couldn't make out most of the time. Ending up chewing on one of my ears with her teeth (lightly)! As we started walking away.

What a shame, Charles never got the attention and womanly play, of this wonderful creature, who was really here as an exhibit of love and passion, for which I was chosen to receive

Di was a very affectionate women, and I asked her once, "How she could be so responsive with me in that way, as much as she was?"

And she just said 'It's natural, and automatically a part of us, honey – if there is no real love, that won't be there either.'

Di, was a unique woman and person, as we all knew!

How fortunate I was for her to come in to my life as Di or Ethel,

if in fact, they are the same to me.

And now herein we want to relate to Rich and Ethel's first sighting and meeting, as it was great.

CHAPTER EIGHT

We herein, offer testimony of Rich and Ethel's phenomenal "Love at First Sight" - 'Reasons' or on account – in explaining for you, of this below Epic and true romantic story, for your resolution in the belief of Love at First sight.

In 1958, Rich at 18, was a young handsome robust man and a soldier at that time, out to save the world in doing his part for his country by serving in the military.

He of course had many plans for his future life of what he wanted out of it. After joining America's military for the third time then, for a four year hitch, now in the U.S. Air Force...

But before this, originally - Rich quit or just left school by just leaving after a fighting incident and got into the military, lying about his age. He and several of the five school buddies all just walked from the school, planning to never return and didn't.

They, all five went off with the plan of Joining the military and lie about their ages in the U.S. Navy and all got in. As then men were needed for Vietnam, and checking them out as thoroughly wasn't a real priority to the military at that time. After all his initial twenty six week basic training (bootcamp) in Bainbridge Md, and so on, was over, he was sent to the U.S. Naval Academy at Annapolis Maryland to start serving in a variety of duties, as a deck hand on the USS Cainman "Hunter-killer" class, submarine, currently in port for repair's and so on.

As well, also then assigned as an honor guard at the academy in the meantime, from his ship, until the USS Cainman was ready for service.

And then in the meantime, I was later assigned in a Landing party during the Vietnam war era, spending less than a year, after the Navy learned he and his buddies all lied to get in, when one was killed and another lost a leg.

Rich's buddies later told the Navy, all were underage and had no parental permissions. All were later honorably discharged and recommended highly for their service, telling them to come back again when you're old enough, in our Navy.

And so, after his then current - year hitch, would be over in the Air Force at age 21, Rich was contemplating going to California   a n d becoming a motorcycle cop on the California Highway Patrol, and so on. (But of course, it never happened because his life changed dramatically after meeting Ethel.)

Relating in this book, at that time, Rich had no vision of having a girlfriend or being married, but I suppose that's how day dreaming does things.

But in reality - here, his future plans were totally different – no girlfriend and definitely no wife then.

Although his 'Love at First sight came into play almost immediately, after his very first visual contact with Ethel, and gained momentum as time went on, thinking about everything.

While Rich was serving in the Air Force this time, he met Ethel Eason at 19, for the first time, while marching in a military parade in New York, that he really didn't want to be in, and fought hard to get out of it, but couldn't.

And had he gotten out of the parade, chances are he and Ethel wouldn't have ever met, and their two wonderful children of course, "wouldn't be here." He didn't get out of the parade and then went on with it!

He had congregated near some bars and restaurants in the busy downtown area, where he and most other soldiers were hanging out trying to hit on all the girls nearby.

Rich was not a drinker, and basically just hanging out as well, looking at the ladies, with all his soldier buddies...

Most of the girls were from a large church that came to watch the parade. Later we learned that Ethel was a child of Christ, and avid follower and another reason she was in fact there, at the parade.

There were hundreds of people at the parade and a lot of noise and so on. People everywhere bumping into one another and so on. Then suddenly

Rich heard his sergeant blowing his whistle for his men to assemble to fall in line position to get into the parade, as it was preparing to start.

Most of his buddies were running and so on to get back to the formation. There was a large gathering of girls, near where Rich had been standing and they were being sort of pushed out of the way of the military men trying to get back with their formation, and as they were hurrying, bumping into the girls and lightly pushing them out of the way of the soldiers were hurrying to their command.

I would say right in the immediate area Rich was standing maybe a hundred or so women, being forced nicely out of their way as the soldiers were running.

I was one of those guys trying to get back with my formation, along with the rest of them, and not really looking to hard at them, as I was rushing by. And at one point myself and a couple other guys sort of pushed this smaller group of girls to the side, and a few fell down.

Still in a rush, but myself and another soldier helped a few girls up and out of our way, "they were all pretty" I didn't get to look very hard, but one of the girls I helped up and out of the way I later learned was Ethel, but never found that out at that time, for sure ...

She had a beautiful face, with a loving smile from ear to ear, and gorgeous eyes, pretty long dark hair, and so polite. Continuously apologizing for being in my way, and then. . . she was up and gone!

I finally got back to my company and got in formation, I repeatedly looked over toward her, to try and get another glimpse of her, and finally saw a little feminine arm waving in my direction, hopefully meant for me, and I waved back, not knowing if it was Ethel or not.

As our company started marching to the beat of the parade, I again looked over in the direction the girl was in, and could see her sort of tip toeing up and down, waving, and of course I waved back, still not knowing really who it was, or if the girl was acknowledging to me or the guy next to me, but I kept waving anyway.

We then must have marched some thirty blocks or so, and I periodically saw the same girl jumping up occasionally and waving in my direction, again not really knowing if it was for me or she was just waving at the parade or another guy.

The parade continued on another five or six blocks, when it started raining pretty hard, and of course most spectators were scurrying off to dryer areas, and most of the soldier's broke ranks running every which way to avoid the rain!

I then said to myself, self, there we go, she's gone – I couldn't see her anywhere and I was heart-broken, thinking I'll never see her again –another time 'November Rain' for my bad luck.

By this time, everybody had scattered, I searched and searched for her, but no luck, and finally gave up and left the area, and knowing little to nothing of New York, I was not from this area, not sure where to go, but a few of my buddies were heading to the local USO club for shelter and whatever, so I went along.

Thirty minutes or so later, we were inside the USO having coffee and so on. Was a lot of people there, most of which were women, my buddies started hitting on the girls and playing ping pong and so on, I just found a good chair and sat down, still looking for the girl I was interested in.

A few hours later, still sitting near the entrance door, several girls came into the USO and were standing by the door talking to some of the other hostesses, when I noticed one girl, that really did look like the one I wanted and had been looking for, but still uncertain.

I later learned Ethel was a new hostess there, and this was only her second time there, so she stayed by the door greeting people, if that was her.

The gal I thought was her was really pretty, and very nice to everyone, especially all the young soldiers - which was the reason she was there.

I'm sitting there watching her all this time, as she's greeting and talking, "and I started day dreaming again" about what it would be like to be with her, and maybe even married to her!

I was on cloud nine then, not understanding why I was thinking this way all the sudden, and not even realizing I was!

As I was day dreaming, I made up my mind, I, was going to marry her!

Hell – I hadn't even met her yet, didn't know her name or anything, she might have a boyfriend or even already be married!

I had sat there all this time thinking and day dreaming about her, and let myself fall in love with her!

Well, then I got up, and headed over to introduce myself and get to know her, right then and there, assuming she was the one, not worrying about any other guys who wanted to be with her, tonight while she was hosting at the USO club.

I walked right up to her and introduced myself to her, and the first thing she said back to me then was –

'Oh, I know you, I saw you marching in the parade today' – 'Where did you run off to when it started raining', she said she tried to find me, she remembered me bumping into her, knocking her down earlier.

She said she tried to get my attention when I was marching in the parade – "WOW, then that was you and you were waving to me?"

Then she said 'Yes', and "I've been here for the last few hours watching you, to see if you were the same girl."

She then went on to say, 'I never saw you sitting there, and I have really been looking for you. I wanted to meet and see you also. I'm really glad we finally met up.'

I gave her my name, and then she put her hand out, I thought for me to shake, but she then grabbed my forearm caressing it, as she said 'Hello, I'm Ethel and really glad we found each other finally.' Telling me then she felt heartbroken, loosing me in the rain today, as well.

"My buddies that were with me, went on to meet other girls there and I was going to take you home when we left." And she agreed to that!

In the meantime, Ethel who was just 19, then told me she lived at home with her parents and two brothers, and a sister, had a job as a secretary for the Glens Falls Insurance Co.

Actually, she had a second thought before meeting me, to introduce me to her younger sister Claire, as Ethel was a year or so older than Rich thinking I may have been too young for her.

But it didn't take long for me to convince Ethel, "No that's never going to happen."

"I want you and this is my plan", and Ethel quickly agreed. After being there and talking to her for a while. We both realized quickly, there could never ever be anyone else.

Ethel and I really knew we were meant for each other. And I offered a ring to her within three months.

Couldn't do it any sooner, as I had no money to buy a ring. I was only making $89.00 a month from the Air Force.

After several months dating, I earned enough money doing odd jobs, to buy a little ring. And then asked her to marry me!

At first, she said "No." Thinking maybe it was too soon for me to make that decision, but "believe me" it wasn't!

Ethel thought about it for about two weeks, and then said O.K. and we got engaged setting our wedding date for that of August 3rd in 1956. And within a year Rich was deployed to Libya, North Africa. Wouldn't you know!

After marrying we lived together for over twenty-five years, until Ethel got sick and passed away. In all that time, I never ever heard her say anything bad about anyone. We had two children Richard Jr, and Beatrice, both wonderful kids.

I was far from perfect, but took good care of Ethel and the children, loving them then and now. Rich of course was Uneducated, but with all my past military training, became a successful private detective.

Ethel died in my arms, while kissing me at 3:30 in the morning, While I was by her bed side in the hospital. Then suddenly started raining horribly, with a great thunder bolt and down pouring- and at that time I knew, this was it, and she took her last breath while kissing me. I left the hospital walking in the rain on November 26, 1982, knowing Nothin' Last Forever. But our- Love will go on and on!

Then I finally left Ethel there at the hospital thinking to myself, if it were up to me, I would never let her go." But she was such a great lady and a child of Christ. I got thinking, because she was still so young l. Maybe God had plans for her helping the rest of the world and us and needed her because of everything going on in America and the rest of the world. Amazingly our son was born on the 26th, of September the following year 1957.

Then I thought to myself, how lucky I've been, to have had Ethel and our loving relationship, with two wonderful children.

And I got home from North Africa, like I promised Ethel, that I would be there at home by the day our baby was due, and then watching my son Richard born, and getting to hold him, within minutes, as he stared at me … in AWE.

And my health is still good, after all the things and places I have been too, and serving our country three times, luckily still in one piece, I really should be happy, "but without Ethel" that will never happen like that, again.

There is no one that could ever convince me that Ethel and I weren't meant for each other, I fell in "love at first sight", without even knowing her name or anything else, and she winked at me' while marching in the parade, when there were hundreds of other soldiers marching right by me, side by side.

She had already made up her mind, it was me, she wanted when she winked. And when the first opportunity came, for Ethel to meet up with me, the first thing out of her mouth was

'I know you' and I tried to find you, searching for hours, but the rain ruined it all.' It was Love at First Sight, and it never ever changed, married on August 3, 1957 for over 25 years.

Rich's personal opinion as to LOVE AT FIRST SIGHT

"I believe all the world should know, that "Love at First Sight" in my opinion is Not just a one- time occurrence – which I will further explain. So, be happy!"

"The Fact that - I, Rich actually met different ladies in my life time, after she died,that I felt in those first moment's, I wanted to be with them in my heart, forever: – That has to be temporary "Love at First Sight" and I knew it each time then. . . instantly."

"While I have been with a lot of wonderful ladies, through the years I never got that feeling with any others" like the two times I had with Ethel and Diana.

"And Princess Diana, in my first meeting with her at the Echoe restaurant, in Cincinnati, I was shocked and flabbergasted at the same time, thinking Diana was maybe Ethel, at first!"

"To me – Diana was so much lik Ethel, in her likeness, demeanor and personality, and 'everything else' – just unbelievable to me! Didn't know if I should scream or hug her. I feel, in meeting her then, prompted this 'realistic coincidence, and I felt causing, the connection with Ethel-Diana, in our Love at First SIGHT right then and there."

CHAPTER NINE

Rich of course was hired by Princess Di, to attempt finding a kidnapped eleven-year-old wrongfully taken to America by the Bio-Dad, during a Domestic dispute, as I previously said in this book. Probably with the intent to never return the child.

Di's heartbroken, endearing friend -turned to Di for her help!

Then plans were in process to venture to America and get the child, secretly, with Princess Di and her hired private eye.

As well, not announcing this trip or venture to the world or anyone else. Di, never advised or told her personal security or body guards as to what she was doing. If she had, in them knowing what she was planning, it would have been aborted.

But Di was legendary in Caring for people in general. And Di would somehow do it and moving forward to honor her word to her very best friend, that she would bring the child back!

In this particular instance, Di, was called and approached by her childhood best friend, for help. At the time, her friend had been treated and institutionalized for drug and alcohol addictions over the kidnapping. Di was in total fear, her friend would kill herself, as she had already tried twice.

Princess Di pledged she would find and bring the child home.

Because her friend's eleven-year-old child, had been kidnapped two years earlier from the home in England by the child's biological father. The biological father had never been married to her but they were living together for over ten years and were now separating.

The Bio-Dad was an American who was from **Cincinnati, Ohio**. But, Di's friend had since, met and fell in love with another man. Then after a domestic dispute, as a result, in her wanting to marry him. The Bio-Dad was mad, wrongfully taking the child and fled to America. Princess Di and her friend were more like sisters, and very close. And she had been in constant contact with Di through the years, keeping Di aware of her situation almost on a daily basis. Further explanation in this book as to the endearing friendship.

At this point in life, Princess Di, herself was in turmoil as she and Prince Charles were in the process of a long-drawn-out divorce. They were Separated, but still living and staying there in the palace, no longer as husband and wife.

Di and Charles were not together as husband and wife during this time, although Di was still in the Palace, separately. But coming and going alone, unquestioned,

Rich for as long as wanted.

But Di had been keeping her distance from Charles and most everyone involved in this long-drawn-out divorce situation.

In view of this, it gave Di a lot of free time on her hands, giving Di the unquestioned missing time needed to go to Cincinnati, for however long it might take or be needed?

Di's butler would lie and cover her missing in action, times and dates, if needed! As well, he frequently was disappearing, off and on himself. Di said 'The fact that, no one knowing where he was at times, along with where I was!'

Di thought, he had some kind of questionable affair going, as well. That he had to mis-lead officials of the Palace about, when asked, so Di told me about.

Di, immediately commenced plans, to organize her attempted recovery of the child, and in helping her, get her kid back to the UK.

In the meantime, told her friend 'I am going to help.'

Di, had told her friend if she got her life back together from her addictions, she would help, get her kid back, as Di was afraid, her friend would commit suicide again, should she not.

The attempt was urgent and meant everything to Di., and very obviously known.

So, when Di, realized she had a perfect time opportunity and the ability to help, knowing Di, she wouldn't let that go and commenced doing it right away.

Di, started making plans to pick her friend up, and the both of them sneak in to America with some other help, and attempt to locate and get the child back.

And secretly Di, started getting everything in motion, and planning to make the trip to America, with her, and a male confidant X Royal Air Force, pilot flying them out secretly.

Through the help and assistance of an administrative aide at the Prime Minister of England's office, Di, had a lady confidant friend working there whom had made contact with American authorities to do a little research in tracking the Bio-Dad's past, down and local address there.

And as well, find a one man "Inquiry Agent" or better known in America, as a Private Detective. Someone who is well regarded in the investigative business, along with an effective defensive ability in his reputation as a black ops body Guard- type, sort of to speak, to protect Di from any harm in case, while working on it.

The source later responded in referring Rich McDonough, a one man operative with an effective back up. A former three-time military man, and trained specialist in wiretap and ops.

Di's plan was to be flown to America in a small, four-six place private plane, by another close confidant, an x Royal Air Force pilot, and close friend of Di', who in the past, once gave Di, pilot lessons.

An experienced person who knew of the trip flying in to the south of England, to change to another small plane and fly directly into Florida, and onward in America.

It will be unscheduled, with no flight plan, with unknown, scheduled landing at the small private-public field known as Lunken Airport in Cincinnati, Ohio USA.

After they land, at about seven AM, Di will call Rich at his office, for an early meet. Princess Di called around 7am from a pay phone in the Hyde Park area of Cincinnati, Ohio USA. Rich's phone rang several times before answering, as he was eating breakfast then, with greasy hands from holding some cold Popeye's chicken, saved from last night. But when it rang again, he of course answered, when I did answer, the caller had such a low sounding female voice with an English accent. Hard to understand and I asked her to "Say that again".

And Rich, had to ask her to "Call back and repeat it." When she did, telling Rich she was Princess Diana of Wales, and Rich kinda, like not believing her and almost hung up in disbelief, but continued to listen to the caller this time...

And Di did repeat it by saying, 'I'm sorry, I talked to softly, so here goes again...' – and this time Rich, heard her loud and clearly when she repeated in saying.

'Hello, this is Princess Diana of Wales calling for an appointment to have a sit-down consultation as soon as possible this morning, as you were referred to me, from the Prime Minister's office in London'...

Well, as I said in the 93 book I wrote then, at first, I thought maybe the caller was a phony bullshitter, probably one of my friends just trying to jazz me with the call.

Well, I played along with the caller, when actually it might have been for real, so I asked what she needed and she then responded by asking to meet up with her in person as soon as we could, I then said O.K. could meet you in 30 minutes. I then hung up and heading out to meet her, of course at a mutually agreed location of the Echoe restaurant in Hyde Park.

Rich, thinking, we will see If she is a phony, they usually won't show up, but I wanted to check it out anyway. After I told her what I looked like, she just said, she would find me, don't worry about it. Later, I'm thinking that was strange, because if she had never seen me, how would she know and then gave me a brief description of her and how she was dressed, then, saying 'See ya!' Rich, in thinking her attitude was weird. I was there in 15 minutes looking for her, but not seeing anyone, looking like what I expected, thinking the caller was a phonie.

Suddenly a women tapped my shoulder, and as I turned to see her in person, the woman was staring right at me, 'eye to eye' and saying hello, reaching to grab my forearm.

"Then as she was caressing my forearm telling me she was Princess Diana . . . hummm. . . I scuffed".

My first thought then, was "WOW" ... "but not out loud!"

"We had never met before" as Rich is now seeing Di for the very first time, of course – but, not considering TV or other publications.

In which I may have seen her, and if I did – I don't remember.

"And believe it or not Rich was absolutely shocked in the way Princess Di, looked".

"Then, he got an immediate closeness vibration from this woman" – as though he had known her forever, and as well a feeling of a family tie, connection from all avenues to this woman, claiming to be that of Princes Diana".

Up and above all this, there was an uncanny similarity, and likeness to that of Rich's wife, Ethel who had passed away at age 43, in November 1982.

Rich was flabbergasted, - looking at this woman, who's saying she was Princess Di, then.

Rich Could hardly believe seeing what he was looking at and thinking to himself, in this person claiming to be Princess Di.

"This woman, claiming to be Princess Di was amazing to me. Yet of course, I did believe her, so far."

Even with all of the similarities, of my deceased wife, and now because, I was immediately attracted due to this powerful exuberance, as to whomever she was"… maybe because of her beauty, I just didn't know!

But, if this wasn't Princess Di, she should be, as she looked like a princess.

As her mannerism was that of a Princess, and I will never forget her perfume - fit for Royalty, with a classical aroma, of sweet Roses, and with an essence of seduction in the fragrance, Wow!

Before all of this incident took place, I had never ever thought about Ethel, in resembling Princess Di, just never thought about that, nor had I ever met or seen Di, before today!

Which was another good reason I couldn't compare the two, of them, then.

But actually, now - I can see a heavy likeness possibilities, as I'm seeing and thinking about it.

But now, since this took place and I have had a good look at this Di, I do feel there certainly is a lot of resemblance, and a definate possibility as to a coincidental resemblance and or likeness, relative to Ethel.

But - I just don't know –

I suppose it's just an amazing coincidence, other-wise!

"Just couldn't believe it!"

As she looked me straight in the eyes, smiling, clutching my forearm at the same time. In saying hello, - And my late wife's absolute demeanor!

And as I thought about this, when I first met Ethel, years ago – I reached out to shake her hand, but Ethel reached over and grabbed my forearm before I could shake her hand, then saying hello – exact same manner!

Just as Princess Di, just did to me when she and I first met, humm!

She (Di) just did the same thing, in that - when we were just then getting introduced.

"I was stunned, looking at her for a short while. But I made no comment as to what I was thinking, right then."

CHAPTER TEN

"Because of the shock in what just happened, as I was looking at her,(Di) - while being introduced, I then, purposely changed the subject matter of our conversation, trying to clear my mind" and thinking, asking to this Di, of details about the kidnapping.

"And then as I started talking to this Di, about her kidnapping case, to change the subject of our conversation primarily to help clear the air in my mind, so to speak of the freaky coincidental likeness, and the woman telling me she is Princess Di."

'The new client Di, then started telling me about the wrongful kidnapping, and why she chose me, was because I came highly recommended through a female confidant working in the Prime Minister's office in London'.

"Of course, I was really happy Di was sent to me. I then wanted to spend as much time with this lady, claiming to be that of Princess Di, as I could," in deciding on several issues. And other facts of the kidnapping that this Di was claiming.

I'm now still thinking maybe this is or was just "coincidence" after meeting, seeing and talking to her, I just "didn't know", and of course, putting my thoughts aside for a while.

And believe me, I'm leaning toward this woman, to in fact actually be Princess Diana – even though she has the likeness of Ethel.

What else could I do, now?

Then I felt, if this Di and I were later working together on her kidnapping case, we would or should get some kind of satisfaction as "to this 'Di's real identity' if this wasn't a coincidence!

Still Not sure, but because Di's demeanor and resemblance made Rich feel somewhat uncomfortable talking to this Di. As there may be more to all this, than he knew.

"What?"

Rich thought, it was 'kind of' - like a 'spirit' drawing Di and Ethel together, 'If this was possible' there's gotta be an explanation.

From my 1993 book, we had now only selected a few chapters of those incidents of dangers Di was in then, that is now reflected in this current book, titled: Princess Diana and her Private Eye

The new book now being published, indicated it will soon be hitting the streets, hopefully in the fall, December of 2022.

"The most Dangerous Encounters from the 1993 book are mentioned herein the new issue, but in much more detail.

In 'Consideration' in talking about our affair back then, we felt if we didn't mention about it in this issue wouldn't give a good explanation maybe making it look bad, or we were trying to hide the reason we have talked about it now.

The cause of the connection in the investigative closeness was a deciding factor for the both of us – 'so we were unsure'. Maybe We just had to much worry and stress then.

We decided to elaborate a little more about it, in the following below pages.

CHAPTER ELEVEN

———— ❦ ————

SO NOW, afterword's of that affair, as to what (Di and Rich) "were thinking in telling", about it or not?

Where – ever, were we going to go with this?

Knowing later it would somehow come out'.

We didn't care - at that time. It had no meaning, other than, us just being together, ...so 'forget it'.

Princess Di, now in reflecting her life, as that of a 'World Leader', along with her legendary life style, in the United Kingdom.

Who was thought of then, as "The People's Princess."

And then, what about Rich - just a lowly private eye. Twelve years older, than Di, and living in America, and Cincinnati, at that!

With nothing to offer Di, except all his love, gratitude, and undying, caring. Allowing Rich, to be a part of this great woman's life.

And later this memory, should be considered a tribute to "America", for Rich helping Princess Diana, another world leader, and an ally for the United Kingdom in the dangerous recovery of a kidnapped child!

Princess Diana Risking herself to personally go, with Rich - a brave protector from America while the two of them risked their lives doing another legendary act of Princess Di, continuing to be the People's Princess, the kidnapping had been successfully thwarted.

'The generated closeness and Love between Di and Rich, was caused between them in light of the dangerous assignment resulting in their constant closeness needed to be successful for the recovery and safety of the kidnapped child along with the constant stress in highspeed vehicle chases and the dangerous villains, of narcotic dealers, and murderers, they pursued was reflected.

A Remarkable

We previously wrote in this book and told of Coincidence of a Possible Reincarnation between Princess Di and Rich's deceased Wife Ethel, that is evident in this novel, possibly reflecting believability at the discretion of the Readers! **Book"**

CHAPTER TWELVE

─────────────── ❦ ───────────────

By the way, "Di, got her small tattoo inscribing 'Rich loves Di Soul mates forever." Di, in telling Rich she had it put on, while they were working in Louisville, Kentucky surveilling the subjects Bio-Dad and the child. Princess Di seemed a little upset later without Rich's presence not being there when it was done.

As Rich was still working on the same case, but elsewhere.

One of the reasons we withheld those questionable incidents from that 1993 book, was due to the 'overplay' on occasion for Di's safety, we didn't want to get everyone all nervous of our moves, or any further dangerous risk taking by Di.

And as well, still not sure if the affair should have been told then for those reasons, because of that.

Hopefully in this book now, it will give a better idea of all the risky more dangerous situations in which Di, and I had been exposed to, then in following the Drug King Pin, in that time.

And if you really think about Di and Rich's affair – in their very first meeting and contact, they somehow felt and knew of that exuberance for one another, in that connection, that they were really meant for each other right then and there!

As well, don't ever forget, it was probably connected to Ethel, if that coincidence or reincarnation mentioned in this book earlier had any meaning or value to it all.

Similarly, Ethel and Rich fell in Love before Rich even knew her name "Love at First Sight" and their story of which - to show, is also included in this publication, for you to reflect on how each, were so alike, when it comes to the claims of "Love at First Sight."

In the times, that Rich and Di were conducting surveillance on the Bio-dad, Rich kept a pretty close observation on Di, by being with her almost continuously for her safety.

And because Rich always seemed to be there for Di, reflecting caring and apparent closeness, was probably because they were falling in love then.

And Rich's concerns then spoke more loudly in his actions for without realizing it.

Along with other unmentioned reasons of Di's that so far had not been told or indicated yet by Princess Di.

Later her personal reasons, all this time, Di was ashamed to admit a longer relationship with the bio-dad, in an effort for Di to talk to him about him stealing the formula.

On stake out's the closeness of the two of us together watching and working the surveillance case took the boredom out, but also "allowing us to do whatever" and in being in love - we had the general idea then.

Of course, this was only providing false pretense to those spectators watching us, as to why we were, hugging and kissing in doing these things. Was an effort to convince watchers, this was our real reason to be out there, acting the part. So, to speak and originally that was true and done to keep suspicions down

Most were thinking that because we were doing surveillance and acting, "was the reason" we were always hugging, kissing and so on, was our real reasons we were actually doing it. But later, as well, I'm sure we would have been doing it even if not on the case – and hopefully that was what Di and I were hoping viewers would think – O.K. with us. But as well, there was NO doubt - "WE WERE IN LOVE."

We have had agents, that couldn't do this type of surveillance, because their better half's not wanting them to do it. Jealousy!

In talking about some of our married agents that had a problem with this part of the job of surveillances, some would quit first, as their partner never liked that.

Di, was a great a conversationalist, and an avid observer, we both loved every minute being together. I suppose because of our feelings mostly, but her safety was paramount in Rich's mind and he, as well never seemed to want to separate, while on the stake outs, even if only for a short while.

It's also my feeling, because of the connection we had for each other, was almost as though, we couldn't seem to separate.

Our closeness on those stake out's I'm, sure, were one of the main causes of our 1993 love affair, and why our love really bloomed, in that somewhat 'short span of time.

CHAPTER THIRTEEN

———— ⌖ ————

Rich felt these were the main reasons why we got connected and ultimately fell in love, "besides my personal feelings thinking maybe I finally found Ethel in Di". The coincidence.

"And at the same time, this was the basic reasons why Di and I, felt their maybe some type of spiritual connection in Ethel, as to why Di connected in the coincidental causes, in our Love".

"But I'm also certain, any man would have fallen in love with Di, under those conditions even without that coincidence of Ethel."

I'm briefly covering the 1993 book written by myself Rich.

"I do, in fact feel I'm an extremely lucky man, to have been involved in this epic story, relative to the manner it all has come down, from our 1993 encounter, as Princess Di's Private Eye!"

In which our Love happened, because of my business connection on the successful kidnapping case.

'Had that not happened Di and I would have never met, I'm sure."

In the forthcoming pages, Di, goes into some details about the girls outing that evening at the infamous So-Ho, and the relationship with the Bio-Dad for all those other times in which earlier Di withheld from Rich, as she was embarrassed to admit it, in telling Rich.

Di, says that she, and five girlfriends all recently had graduated from school, and they all decided to go out that evening celebrating, and always wanted to know what the Infamous "So Ho" underground club in London's downtown area was all about, and we all went there that evening to find out! And that was where they both met the Bio-Dad and later got involved with him. Di now felt it was time to come clean and told Rich why she took those chances going out each time.

Di, admitted to dating the Bio-Dad only a few times back then, off and on, but now gives a later admission that she actually saw him for several months off and on and she ended the relationship because of his drug use and excessive sexual advances, which she continuously rejected.

And she finally hooked her friend up with the Bio-Dad, at her girlfriend's continuous insistence. And within a short time, she was pregnant by him.

Di, later told Rich that she was "ashamed now" because of the important facts, she withheld from Rich at the time she hired Rich to do the kidnapping assignment, back in 1993, by not disclosing that she (Di) actually had, had a closer relationship with the Bio-Dad than she cared to admit to, then.

And probably was the main reason he had the opportunity to steal her notes, when they were on dates, or visiting her.

So, now Rich, learning of this about her and the Bio-Dad, Rich had a better idea as to why Di, was always out there trying to help was really that she wanted to be sure and get to talk to bio-dad about what he did in taking her confidential formulas for the weight control products. Besides that, he was advertising that Di was an advocate for the product, "is not" true and never was!

And this was another reason she took so many risky chances, in working on the kidnapping case, insisting on going with Rich every time and not just because she was fearless. I think in the beginning when she and Rich started working on the kidnapping and probably may have been another reason why Di, always wanted to be near Rich, to be sure she knew if or when the Bio-Dad was seen, later coupled with the beginning of our love for one another.

As Rich and Di were constantly together. The two of them took a lot of chances in pursuing the bio-dad and all types of very risky situations of high-speed chases and such, together fourteen - eighteen hours together daily, working, eating and staying together in the surveillance vans, so as to be on the case continuously.

I mean this type scenario for Princess Di, was so far above and beyond for such a great, beautiful lady, But Di never wavered ever. Always ready, having total concern for the child and her best friend's welfare.

Di, had fear in her mind that her friend would commit suicide if we failed, but we kept on pushing.

And she (Di) wanted to be there then to confront him about stolen personal papers, the formula and documents he took from her, the bio dad claiming Di sponsored his unapproved and dangerous invention-products, using the formulas from that stolen booklet, along with a unique drug he claimed would enhance the lives of the product users – mostly older people.

Di was risking her life, to get that product out of the bio-dad's hands, "to save" the people he could care less about.

Her admission to all this came after a long period of time, while Di and Rich were staked out on the surveillance of the Bio-Dad, and talking for hours, and hours.

While Di and her friends were still in the So-Ho, many men and woman approaching them both with all kinds of gesture's and offers, not to mention an array of every kind of drugs known.

As, well were approached by none other than the Bio-

Dad, otherwise later known to them as the Bio-Dad, hitting on both Di and her friend, besides living with Di's dear friend, was a frequent patron of the So-Ho, a really dangerous man.

Di, said the Bio-Dad and both of them hung out together while there. He and Di, sort of got hooked up, as he really liked Di. They danced to a lot of the music, and listening to all phases of the be-bop and so on, sorta having a pretty good time, while periodically he and Di's dear friend sort of hit it off as well. But Di was pretty sure, he was much more interested in her, Di best friend.

Of course, neither Di or her had any interest in any of the drug paraphernalia or anything like it. There were hundreds of people down there, sort like under the city, and uncontrolled by law enforcement, as there was absolutely no police protection, along with a variety of degenerates and other scumbags so to speak, along with the Bio-Dad.

Not a great place to hang out or ever even think about going back to. Di was thinking they needed to get out of there after a few hours, and when they did Bio-Dad, went with them, thinking maybe he would want to be with Di some more and they all left.

Over a few dates in time, with him, Di decided not to see him any longer, as he was a user of several different drugs and other things, and over aggressive sexually with her, and she didn't like that either.

But in what she said about that, Di, did more than she wanted, then and ended their dating and time together.

A few weeks later her friend became aware that Di, hadn't talked about him in a while, nor had she seen them together, asking Di, what was going on with that.

Di then told her, Bio-Dad was not someone she wanted to know, and didn't like his life style and ended their relationship because of it.

A few days later, she kept asking Di, if she would hook her up with him, as she thought he was cute and wanted to go out with him.

Di refused for some time, but after constantly begging Di to introduce her to him, she did – but warning her what she might be getting into.

She and him started their relationship after a few days, and they hit it off pretty good, in becoming their study date.

A few months later they got an apartment together, and were together over ten years, without ever getting married and she got pregnant right away with their son. Before Di and he broke up, they apparently were a little closer than she wanted to be with his constant aggressiveness and she didn't want to be with him any longer. The kidnapped child was the same age as Di's son William born about the same time.

And was another reason Di, really didn't want her to be with the bio-dad. But during the short span of time Di had seen him, she told him a few things about her personal life, like how she managed to keep herself so vibrant, pretty and slender.

On a few of her dates with him, she gave him a little secret as she called it, about her weight. As well, told him that earlier in her life she had a problem with weight and bulimia.

Di told him, that there in the Palace, they had developed and perfected some kind of a procedure or method for maintaining weight, through some kind of dietary supplement with medical ingredients, that has been working for most who used it for a long time, and she was an avid user, and look at me, she says.

At that time, the Bio-Dad was almost out of medical school, and a constant user of drugs, but - not debilitatingly.

He asked Di, for that recipe but she wouldn't give him any more, than she already had – as he told Di, that what she told him so far, he would apply that to some of the habit forming drugs and sell it on the market. It Will make millions!

After Di heard this from him, she stopped telling him anymore about it, and he was really upset, because he kept telling Di, if they made a product with it in the application he would use, they would get rich fast. And that was another of Di's reason to end her relationship with him, and why she constantly was searching for him, taking all the risk that Rich was taking looking for the child.

And after Rich and Di had found and got the child back from the bio-dad, Jer my brother learned from the child that the Bio-Dad had been working on some kind of a new product to do what he told Di. But so far had not gotten it going. My brother Jer in talking to the child about the product, but Rich didn't ever get to talk with the child then personally, as he was staked out outside making sure everything was safe, when the Bio-Dad told Jer while they were together waiting in the parking garage

This was another of the main reasons, why Di wanted to go along with Rich, besides searching and finding the child, as Di, wanted to get that formula away from Bio-Dad, before he kills someone, and has her name associated with the product.

Thinking in Di searching around she may see what he is doing, and how to destroy his efforts, as another thing not really known was, that formula - has a dangerous side effect that could cause brain cancer, according to the lab research that had been done on it, and told to Di.

But the Bio-Dad doesn't know that, nor would he care, as long as he is making the money from it. further went on to say, that one of the labs they used for several products, recently went up in flames, but the child wasn't sure if it was from Meth or this health supplement.

The child did hear, that the Health supplement, Bio-Dad was working on then had drugs in it, that make you sick or causes death, and Di needed to find out so she would blow the whistle on it, to the UK government, to stop the Bio-Dad.

Previously, while Di and Rich had broken into his Louisville, small plant, Di picked up on hazardous things of the product charges indicating deaths, from what Di said.

Di's goal, now was to advise those perspective users of the newly developed product that it is bad and not to buy or use it.

Chapter Fourteen

~~~~~~~~~~~~~~~~~~ ✦ ~~~~~~~~~~~~~~~~~~

WE GOT THE CHILD TODAY!

Di and I, did in fact work hand in hand, on a night and day basis, as usual to hit our unwavering target together at that time in 1993.

In our effort to accomplish that goal in finding and recovering the child and how we finally accomplished it, back then.

Writing about part of the recovery now, and the conclusion of taking him from the Bio-Dad, on the spot, further towards the end of this book, in covering more details to show it went down.

We found and took the child with us, right then and there, after the bio-dad allowed the child to stay in the parking lot, while playing basketball with three or four other kids. This was exactly the kind of scenario we were waiting and hoping for. This recovery is and was the best method, getting him, and with no problems.

While the Bio-Dad was inside an apartment visiting his mother, at the known apartments, located at the Kenwood Towers in the Kenwood area of Cincinnati, Ohio USA, Catching the Bio-Dad today was great.

No more High-Speed Chasing! This was where it brought us to.

Where another of our high-speed chases took us today, in the process of our surveillance this in which all the many chase risks, was well worth it.

Through those pages, covers the manner in which we handled taking the child.

Di and Rich had followed the Bio-Dad today, and earlier told us she also just recently learned the Bio-Dad's real last name. Although, now not really important, but for the record. She told us he also uses about four other alias names, as needed.

But on this day, we actually tracked him down and found the child, with the Bio-Dad. We had been following him from the Loft apartments to several locations, and eventually hooking up with a woman driving a red jeep that he apparently knew. And he got into her red jeep and was making out in the front seat, with the woman, while the child was still in the Bio-Dad's car and watching his dad's activities.

The child remained in the Bio-Dad's car then, and we probably could have made an attempt then, but if anything went wrong the Bio-Dad would have been right on us, so we just held off in anticipation of a better chance, that we did shortly later on.

We just sat on the stake out and watched him still, in his Bio-Dad's car. While the bio-dad was doing his thing with the chick in the red Jeep.

There were a couple younger kids in the Jeep with them, and probably why nothing has gone down yet with it, due to the Bio-Dad and the woman their making out in her Jeep.

In commenting a little about the Bio-Dad who took the child, he was dangerous and I felt Di, had placed her life in a bad place, which is why I was so drawn to be closer to Di for her safety.

In saying that this man was a drug dealer in the underworld, of Cincinnati and became a very bad actor, so to speak and rising himself up in one the several mid-western cartels as a king pin, leader.

After we saw the Bio-Dad drive in this large parking lot and area, the Bio-Dad drove in a large circle in the lot checking things out, 'I think,' and finally ended up stopping just by the side of this large apartment building entrance area.

He then backed his van up to the building. Then just sat in his van for a good ten minutes, checking everyone else in the lot, to see what they were driving and how they looked as far as someone attempting to grab the child or even law enforcement checking him out- always very careful.

After the Bio-Dad felt secure in where he was, I suppose that's when he decided to get out and take the child with him, although still looking all around suspiciously, they got out "conservatively" as though watching everyone in the area to see what they were doing,

The child casually dressed and wearing a hooded jacket, walked around to the driver's side and still looking all around, they then drove backwards slightly and edged up to one of the large glass entrance doors, and still looking around pretty hard, as he got out and they went inside, and walked to the elevators.

I'm thinking all these suspicious moves, might have been due to our chase surveillance, in us getting a little too close for him. But mainly because I think the Bio-Dad wanted to be certain it was safe here, before allowing him to play in the parking lot.

Rich was of course watching their every movement, and gave them a little time as they stood in the hall waiting for the elevator to arrive on the first floor, and Rich's precision planning for the Bio-Dad and child to get in to the elevator as the doors slowly opened, Rich got in to the elevator carrying several card board boxes as sort of a gimmick or excuse in getting the same elevator, and acting as though he was having problems carrying them and not really paying any attention to anyone else as the elevators door slowly closed. while the Bio-Dad and child walked just a few feet away and knocking on the door of where they were going, just long enough to let Rich see which apartment, as the elevator moved, to the apartment door number while going further up.

After Rich made the apartment number he gave it a few minutes, buy riding on up to the top, getting out and waiting a few minutes, and then of course getting back in and riding down to that same floor, where of course got off to case it out, and see what ever he could see, along with the apartment number, for sure!

Once Rich checked out the apt number, he saw and older lady about the age of the Bio-dad's mother or something, verified the apt number and kept going. Rich overheard them talking and welcoming them - the lady about sixty-five or so, kissing the child, as they talked and walked from the door. Obviously, the Bio-Dad's mom or whom ever.

The complex here was called the Kenwood Towers, which had over two hundred units, and considered one of the nicest and best in the area.

As Rich passed their apartment he noted a large terrace or balcony where she had apparently been sitting, making note of this to be seen from the parking lot.

Rich headed back to our stake out vehicle, and started checking out the rest of the building and parking area, to see what kind of an observation the mother, Bio-Dad or whom- ever was watching from up on their balcony.

On this day, that we actually found and recovered the child, we had to be really careful, as we observed the Bio-Dad talking with a cop or some type of law enforcement agent, right near where we going to make the recovery.

Don't know for sure what the Bio-Dad was doing, thinking he maybe just telling them, that he thought his child may be getting taken, were not sure at this time. So, we just sat back and waited a short while longer.

Ultimately, we just waited to let them make their first move.

Suddenly the Bio-Dad, got out of his car, and went over to, two men in a black van and told them something, and suddenly they drove off at a high rate of speed, leaving the Bio-Dad there in the parking lot.

The Bio-Dad went into the office, in the building alone, and was in there for about ten minutes, so in the meantime the child was out in the parking lot alone, and our agents told Rich, who headed back to our surveillance van, got in and told them this was apparently the child's grandmother up there, and probably now, is gonna be it!

But they were both still inside her apartment sitting down talking. Rich exclaimed to the rest of his people, he felt this was it, and they were going to head back to their safety haven and wait a while, which is what they did, UNTIL Rich gave the go-ahead.

So, after checking everything out, and they got prepared to make the attempt. Everyone got into one van, and had a last-minute consultation, to make sure everyone was aware that this was the place, and what they were going to do, getting everything understood.

The mom was riding in the van with Jer, Rich driving, and parked very close to the escape van. In the general area. Rich hadn't been with the child and the rest of the crew, as he was checking the parking lot out, in case they had gotten on to us.

We had a last-minute meeting and discussion between the four of us with last minute instructions, as there cannot be any screw ups. Rich continued his observation of everything, the child was in the main vehicle to go with them in getting away, once the move was made.

Rich then, once again explained to Di's, friend who is the mother of the child, that she is the rightful, and legal parent, and she would have to be the one to grab the boy, although we would be right by to assist, if needed.

After sitting here in the lot for some time, watching the child as they played basketball and so on in the complex, at the given and right moment, we call you step out of surveillance unit and call the child, once getting the attention of him that you were here in the lot, and to come to you right now. Once seen you it's done – both of you were then instructed to get into that van, close the door and prepare to be driven off right away, probably at pretty high rate of speed to elude capture.

So, everybody was ready and understood the plan – this was it and we were getting the hell out of there soon as we got the kid.

I personally had to take a lot of extra precautions to keep Di and her, safe, causing more risk and bad times for myself as we were picking the kid up.

Then there was a male witness watching what we were doing and we had to be very careful, who might tell police what they had observed here, and we got the hell out of there.

THEN Rich made the call for us to commence the pickup, and mom immediately got out of her van, stood where the kid could clearly see us, as she was calling to them, who was playing within ten feet of her, and saw and recognized her, calling Mom, and ran to her van, they momentarily hugged and both jumped in the back, slammed the door and Rich started driving out of the lot at a high rate of speed, and on to Kenwood Road.

Rich was driving at a high rate of speed, traffic was somewhat heavy, apparently the Bio-Dad must have spotted us, and gave chase behind rich.

Jer saw this and made a dash to catch up close to Rich's van, and at the next intersection, Jer did a 380 in the street, making a complete turnaround, and was then facing on the opposite side of Kenwood Rd, blocking the Bio-Dad from coming up Kenwood Rd at a high rate of speed, but then was forced to "stop" in his tracks, because Jer had the Kenwood Road blocked, and he had no way to get past him, and Rich continued on without being detected for license plate or description.

Jer, made some excuse to the Bio-Dad, as to what happened with his vehicle, and that was all over then as Rich was booking.

Rich made it on to our safe Haven, ironically only about two miles further up on Kenwood Rd, where our office was located at that time.

Rich made it, hiding our vehicle in the underground parking facility of our office building, and we all waited in the surveillance vehicle for further instructions, while Rich remained on the street checking things out, assuming the child was alright, and ready to go home.

CHAPTER FIFTEEN

The witness that saw us leave the Kenwood Tower, was not a problem and really couldn't help the police.

As we have found that individuals who want to question all that they in-fact learn or see or hear about, in various situations usually have little to no idea what's really going on, and should keep their doubtful questions to themselves. As he, this witness couldn't help police at all. Didn't get our tag number!

So once the Bio-Dad figured mom grabbed the child, and then he (bio-dad) told the police the child had been kidnapped, but of course didn't tell police that, was the Bio-Mom who took the child, so the police would be more on his side.

As well the Bio-Dad, he told the police to set up a 911 quadrant, and stake out Greater Cincinnati Airport to catch them there, thinking that would be our way out - 'but how wrong., they were'! We figured that's what police would do.

But of course, we were flying out of the private airport called Lunken in the Cincinnati, area in a small six place Cessna, with no flight plan and or schedule, from Cincinnati, and not leaving until about midnight, to be sure the coast was all clear first!

Di's pilot, had a made up phony name for Di's pilot. He called Rich, and told Rich he was on the way then and was flying the four of them to Florida, where they would change planes to fly the four of them on to the south of England and back to the Palace, and that was the plan then, and they made it.

So, far were good, and their departure, will be covered further in detail in this book below, Rich and everyone else were all waiting in the parking garage of Rich's office, where they will be until they leave later tonight from Lunken Airport and on their way back to the United Kingdom,

and the case was then over.

Aside from all the explanations of those dangerous times – along, with the FINAL admission of Rich & Di's love affair.

Have faith in: "Love at First sight and coincidences"!

Specific planning is always important, to make the plan and follow it, when possible!

The information supplied – Was by the way, important Information as to specifics from the first book, published in 1993.

Hopefully now giving some facts and information for the new edition published 2022 that was not in that book, are now included: And titled "Princess Diana and her Private Eye"

IN EXPLAINING - There would have been no other reason or opportunity for Di and Rich to have ever met, been together, or fallen in Love.

As their original and only mission - at first, was to find the Kidnapped Child and they did that successfully. Business brings people together many times and always will ... in wonderful ways and experiences, such as this.

"This is why it is so important, to explain the connections between Di and Rich in the current book publication to hit the streets in the Autumn of 2022.

This book was and is attempting to show Di and Rich's time together. With Rich and Di, having this mission to save the child, that was the basic and only reason for them being together.

And of course, Di and Rich were together every day for many hours, trailing the subjects as to where ever they went, then staking them out, and waiting in anticipation to catch the Bio-Dad and the child in the right situation, where we could slip in and grab the child and be gone! ('Long term surveillance - No Other Way')

Making a clean get away – and you know, that's exactly how it finally went down! As told in the concluding pages.

The Bio-Dad was and is a very careful man in knowing, that if the Bio-Mom, ever tries to get the child back from him, it will have to be a very secretive and only a one-time attempt.

Chapter Sixteen

Being as a supplier, added to Rich's worries knowing the bio-dad would not hesitate to kill them, over the child. Rich was aware of the security for the thugs of the cartel and Di's concern in protecting herself and her party involved, but she's was not scared,

Only Determined. I'm sure all of the United Kingdom would be proud of Di, in risking herself for her friend. Another instance as to her legendary reputation in being there, as the People's Princess.

As well Di, felt secure with Rich in the search to recover the child, knowing Rich, would never let anything happen to her, as best he could, and she felt safe.

Of course, Rich was the head investigator and Di' body guard, securing Princess Di and her party in this attempted recovery.

Telling me she and her friend want to be with us all the time, and I agreed then when Di told me that. And because of her desire to be right there with us, then meant she would have to perform the acting out, for the public to see. Having Di with me was great, and I was glad because of our closeness together.

And of course, this agreement was made at the initial time of retaining Rich and the Shamus Agency, and would have been fully honored, even at the cost of Rich's life.

In Further stipulating herself and *friend,* be in our vehicles at all times in the course of searching and or stake outs.

Everything she requested was great and she was advised and knew of all the possible risk in searching, and knew Rich felt great concerns in the responsibility for her, he now had on his shoulders, should anything happen to her.

Our stake outs, high speed chases and possible physical contact or confrontations should it come to that, was Rich's concern, so we went on with the mission as agreed on.

Our plan had been and was, to use two specially equipped vans plain unmarked, with one-way tinted glass, on the sides. Both units fully equipped with two man sleeping facilities, when put down in using. And two radio handsets. Rich driving the chase vehicle as we were doing, and her friend and mother of the child riding in a separate van with my brother 'Jer' who is an agent. Di will be in the lead surveillance unit van, with Rich.

I went on to tell them both that we would be in the field chasing and following the subjects pretty much night and day, that is, until we come up with alternate plan, or find out where the child is some other way and make attempts to snatch him some other way. We told her friend, that once an attempt is made, if it was not successful, and the opposition knows were out there looking to grab the kid, they will take steps to stop us! But knowing there in the drug business, we may have to take other precautions, so I just want to warn and let you know, Di, please stay with me, and don't take any chances.

Maybe if they know where out here, in order to stop us, they could even call law enforcement telling them to be aware of a possible kidnapping of his child and give our description of what they know of us, but they will never tell police, you are the Bio-Mother, to enhance the police to be diligent...

So, law enforcement may shoot at us. Them not knowing who we are, or that you're the rightful Bio-Mother, so the Bio-Dad can keep the boy, maybe getting us arrested.

Not telling police that you're the mom. The chances of any further success for us grabbing the child, is going to be severely hampered, if they get any idea we are after them, that's why this attempt has to be totally secret just like you planned it and this was the total procedure Rich had laid out, and was to be followed to the letter, when we commence our operations.

This is why we had to be very careful and especially on the late-night stake outs, Should Di be with me on a late-night stake out, she must be ready and prepared to try and convince whomever is seeing us together, looking like were just lovers and or whatever! And there was no problem in doing this.

Rich

CHAPTER SEVENTEEN

From here on in, I'll be telling mostly about the times and events myself and Di spent in dangerous situations together with each other, that wasn't included in the 1993 book, and searching for the child, or just spending time being together.

Most of the time, Di - was usually dressed very casually, with jeans, and low-cut tops, and gym shoes, but occasionally wearing heels, as she looked so good wearing them, basically when we spent time together in restaurants.

Of course, Di's selection of clothes was pretty limited, due to the only clothes she brought with her from the Palace.

At one particular time, when Di, went into a small women's boutique with me and bought a silky purple dress, that was somewhat form fitting to her classic figure, she had.

She tried the dress on, and she looked amazing, even more beautiful, if that was possible. The sexy dress she bought, and she later wore came to about 2 inches above the knees, form fitting around her thighs, hips, and rear. Giving Di confidence in the way she looked as that of the young women she was.

She looked marvelous, especially when she walked! She planned to wear it later this evening after she and I quit surveillance for the night, about ten or eleven, sort of checking out the town, bars, restaurants, night clubs...breaking the monopoly of our surveillance routine.

She looked all around the rest of the shop, and also bought a pair of earrings that dangled, about two inches, very pretty and I wanted to pay for it, but she wouldn't let me.

She suddenly pulled me to the side, while kissing on my ear and 'whispered, Let's get a tattoo'!

They have a shop in the boutique, laughing all the time, as we kinda hugged and laughed about it, we walked over to that area, again as we bounced hips while we walked over to it, Di, loved doing that, and so did I.

Di was a marvelous gal' – "all women" but I'm sure she never really let Charles know that, as she said he didn't seem 'interested in much of anything except Camilla, and Di's not sure, why'!

And that's why, in Di's own words - 'Why, He would want to be with her?' Exclaiming 'That old bag, as she is a nothing!'

I then, kiddingly asked if Camilla had any tattoos on her, and Di looked me in the eyes laughing, for a good while, and said – 'Just her face!'

Then exclaimed, again saying, 'Just her face, I don't know.'

'But, honey, I really want to get one with you, please!

To always remember you by.'

"I, then said to Di,- Humm, sounds like I'm going to be out of your life soon"!

Di then exclaimed – 'Well honey, we both knew-we'll never be together again - once I go back to England, unless some kind of miracle happens!'

'I, need Something to always remember you by, but in a spot, that no one will see if I'm undressing!'

'That is, no one but you – Darlin.'

I then asked, "In your position in life, does anyone at the Palace ever have to see you, that they would notice?" …

And she said 'NO, not anyone that I can think of.'

"I then said "What about Charles?" 'She said 'NO.' Emphatically – 'He hasn't seen me that way for a long time and now, he never will again.'

"I then said What about if you have another man, they might wonder about it".

'Di, laughed and said, 'Nope. . .'

'You're my only man. . .'

'And I wish you always were – honey, there will never be another man for me, after being with you!'

I then said, "Do you really want to do this?"

'And Di said 'YES – Oh yes, more than ever'

'I really mean it, sweetheart!'

'Di went on to say 'I have never had one.'

'But then until now, never wanted another man to do it with me!'

'You see, your my soul mate and I love you now, and probably forever.'

'So, what do you think sweetheart?'

'Will you do it with me?'

"Then we kissed, for a long, long time.

"And I told her "Yes." She - got really excited and wanted me to go with her to pick one out.

"And we did".

'With a small heart and our initials in it,' Di, telling the artist how much she loved me, and where she wanted it to be put, "But not allowing me (Rich) to know where at that time."

"After we picked our design out with our inscription and made an appointment for the next evening to come there to have it done".

Di, was so happy, and we left to go eat, put her new dress on and go show her off to the world tonight at the restaurants and bars for a while, "I was so proud of her, who wouldn't be."

CHAPTER EIGHTEEN

---✜---

Earlier this day, we were talking in the front of our surveillance vehicle, while on the stake out when Di, was talking, telling me,

'She just wants to live a little.'

'Saying she gave up her life to be the Princess and basically to bear two 'Heirs' to the throne of England', her children whom she loves dearly.

But she had no personal life, and constantly alone and bored. Like most women her age does, saying she wants to go shopping, more and see and buy things, 'she said she probably would never wear and so on', seeing other young women living.

'And see other people her age, and how they live their lives', go out on the street in public places where everyone goes to.

'She also said, she wants to dress down a little cheaper, to see how it looks and be noticed by everyone, and especially men, as it's important to know she's still desired, that's all'.

'She says, she rarely ever got to go out a lot in the public places, like grocery stores, restaurants or sporting malls, and events, and so on by her self- alone!' Now she is free, and wants that!

'Then reflecting how lonely she was, and has been', not really considering to just be a plain woman, 'but wants to be a looker from now on even if she is never with another man.'

She misses men hitting on her and so on, and wanting them to make dates, giving her "small talk" not that she would ever accept, but just the offer from the guys and so on, letting them all know she's alive'.

'Saying she's not sure she looks pretty anymore'.

"Then she laughs and gives me a kiss telling me, she wished she had met me a long time ago, continuing to hold my hand", squeezing it often as we walked and her laughing as we went on...

"We embraced continuously while walking and talking, bumping our hips together with a rhythm, all the way to go eat, having fun".

"She just wants her normal life back, before she became the Princess."

'To dress like a normal young woman, not all that royalty crap, they all try to push on her, all the time by them'.

Servants all, saying to me all the time, in your position as a princess, you should dress in royalty fashion and styles.

'Di saying 'That's B.S. I should be able to wear whatever I want, I'm the princess -not them! And without someone picking out what I'm to wear'. I mean, to be able to go out at a moment's notice with whatever I have on or choose, if asked.' And so on.

Saying to Rich, 'I just want my life back and to be with someone that really likes me, like you do, and thinks I'm cute, pretty or whatever, and telling me that.'

Di, wants to be able to go into a bar alone or with a girlfriend, sit down and order a drink, and get approached by guys flirting with her.

Even if she doesn't take them, up on their proposals – 'Just the fact that they do it,' tells me, I'm still sought after.'

Just to talk with them, though she may not be with them – but just knowing, she's still got it, You know?

And as we continue walking side by side bumping our hips back and forth together, and loving it, just having fun being lovingly together.

Now Finding our first bar for the evening, to drink and have the greatest Barbeque in Memphis.

And Di telling Rich frequently, she really loves being with him along with my occasional flirting. 'It's all just so natural of Rich, loving woman in his admiring sexy, ways', Di exclaims...

Chapter Nineteen

———— ⌒∞⌒ ————

Di says I always treated her like a real woman, always admiring her, helpful and ready to listen to whatever the woman wants to do or say!

All though, Rich was eleven + years older. Di, thought Rich was a good-looking man, and a probable womanizer, yet still picked him, even though she new Rich was a womanizer, it made no difference to her. Because . . . "You, Di, were totally secure in knowing, that no one else did or would compare to you and Ethel. As you, both coincidentally were one and the same." I then told Di "Lois and I were about the same age spread, and we've been married happily, a long time". Some of Lois's actions are very similar to Di's, but maybe not in the same way.

"As well, Lois also was very beautiful like you Di," and I enjoyed watching other men drink her in, 'so to speak' while their women weren't watching, as their 'man' flirted with Lois, in just walking past her, without them getting much response!

"I, was always so proud of Lois being with me, with all those other guys wanting her, yet it was Me (Rich), she was with".

"Sort of like you Di, being with me. And, 'how well' I knew, you could have been with any man, but chose me!"

Lois was sexy like Di, in her movements.

"And Lois's return responses toward flirting men, towards her, Lois was always, cool and sophisticated, in her, giving the men a negative response looking, back!"

"As in, eat your heart_out."

"Lois giving them that You'll, never be with me, look"

"And Just that uninterested look in general, she gave-back, without saying anything was great!"

"Lois always looked beautiful in about anything she wore, and as well, her looking like royalty, herself most always."

"Lois had great movement in her provocative walk, that most men waited to see, and as well, me!"

"And I still Love, her now."

"I (Rich) have been sort of a womanizer for over twenty years." "And why not? I 'm looking, and been searching, for women- like Ethel types, that's how I found Lois."

"My reason for being a rather active womanizer, was and is my late wife's fault because her death hurt me so much. I've been trying to find her in most all women, I see. "

Di, then asks – 'So, if you miss Ethel so much, and was really hurt, how could you want to become a womanizer'?'

"So, to briefly explain, my reasoning, even though I don't think I was truly a womanizer, just lonely and missing Ethel."

"But hopefully what I'm going to tell you, will explain that a little."

"My wife's death, was so tragic for me. I couldn't bear being without her, ever since, then and even now!"

"I then went on and explained how it all came about."

"It's pretty simple if you really think about it!"

Then in me giving my explanation and reasoning to Di, for this. I told her "If you really think about it – here's my honest answer, which is going to take a little time. due to the complexity – but you must really listen and understand my reasoning."

"Like I said, you think I may be a womanizer, and your right, to some degree."

"But only with hopes at one time, finding a lady that maybe compares to Ethel, such as you."

"But you have to do a lot of searching, woman like her, are few and far apart, if any, are even left!"

"But I don't know about this so far. When Ethel was dying, I promised on her death bed, Honey I'll go on, and try to find another".

"At 3:30 thirty in the morning she died, with my lips on her hers, I'm crying and slobbering all over the place," as I left walking from the hospital out into the cold raining November night.

"I had pledged this to Ethel, because I loved her for so long and she wanted me to do this, in being happy..."

"I loved our life together for over 25 years" and would never get married again, but she told me she didn't want me to do that, or be alone..."

"Saying yes, in wanting me to go on!"

"Ethel saying that she was going to be gone for ever and ever, never to return to our children and good future life together."

"Really after all those years of having little or nothing, to show for how hard we both worked all those years, and me being in my own business over 25 years."

"Then we really just started making it on the good side of life financially, and now Ethel's gone and not here to enjoy it."

"Her never having a chance to enjoy all she and I worked for together all those years. Ethel, was the best."

"While I was standing by her death bed, then suddenly Ethel sort of snapped out of it for a sec and the irregular breathing, stopped."

"She took my hand saying with a very weak voice, "NO Darling" please go on."

"I know that you took good care of me and the children all those years, with all your love and heart, and I want you to go on."

"Please, Honey go on with your life and enjoy what's left, you deserve it."

"Find a good woman, you deserve that. Moments later she died, with my lips on hers, sobbing and sobbing as I walked away leaving her bedside, Ethel lying in her bed and I'm Crying as I walked away, with my face all wet from the tears."

"I miss Ethel so much, I was really lost knowing she was gone..."

"The success in my work, I, was considered one of the best in my business and making a lot of money then, and almost at the top, I could now afford to do and give her anything she ever wanted, everything now. . . but it was too late!"

"As then, Ethel had pretty much everything she ever wanted in me and our children", she said.

"Ethel, was a good person, just a woman with a true and caring heart for her family and life in general, and just normally happy and content most all the time – 'very few like her!'"

"Like most young couples, we had a lot of bad times trying to just make it through the years. But as well, a lot of good times being together."

"Ethel was a great mother, wife and person in general, just like Princess Di, was from what I knew of her."

"Ethel deserved more, that I couldn't provide way back then."

"I, should have been the one that died, because the kids needed their mother more than me."

"But of course that was God's plan and decision."

"Now, I know this will seem to be, or was a long-drawn-out explanation, but an important one! When you look at it, you'll understand me and my reasoning better."

"Because, most men that date, do that a lot, unless they find one lady right away and accept her."

"But if not, they continue searching, and searching, so it's my personal feeling those men are NOT in fact womanizers, but become 'players' for obvious sexual reasons."

"So, you see, I date a lot, but really searching in my quest to find Ethel, or someone like her, is what I'm really looking for and why continuing in my hopes."

"And if or when I do find her, my womanizing will be over. I really don't think I'm a real player, but only a womanizer in sense of the title, but because I was particular, and still looking for Ethel."

"So instead, I'm just searching for that "coincidental women" who was of my specifications of honesty, great company, personality and beauty. Fitting my idea of the women I had in you, so to speak it!"

"While I may have dated often, but I tried not to be a Player as, I'm many times thought to be, but - just desperately searching for that woman."

"So, Di, this is sort of like, our 'Love affair' people are telling me, that you were just a 'coincidence', 'and I don't want to believe that' so I went on with my own beliefs."

"Di, I don't want to be considered a player in your eyes, because, in listening to Ethel's last words, she was absolutely right." Go on with my life, - Ethel told me in her last breath!

Even though I didn't want to get married again, unless I found that person."

"I'm being told, by some that 'you were and are' - just a 'coincidence' and now gone forever."

"So, I say to them just live with it. 'I am'!"

AND THE TIME WILL COME FOR ALL OF US, to know for sure!

Then all the "doubter's" will, see and be in "Aw", as to my time with Princess Diana, bringing satisfaction in knowing.

"While I loved my wife, and I like women".

"And So on, so should I only want to be with a woman in real desperation?"

"I need to try and find a woman who fit's my spec's so to speak".

"And only you, just – 'YOU' Diana have so far!"

"To Princess Di, of course, I'm still really not sure if you were just a 'coincidence', because of your likeness and similarities of Ethel, and along with all our great times being together with you."

"But I do know one thing for sure and for a fact."

When I held you Di, 'physically' caressing and squeezing, I'm satisfied in you, and the 'coincidence', as that of one!"

"I'll always be longing for your touch, with your loving words that always followed each time, that you loved me."

"And Not doubting that for a minute, that you didn't!"

I'm ending this book with thoughts of these words in mind, "whatever" it was I, am and was a very lucky man!

Those of you thinking this was a wonderful story, maybe 'wishing it had been you instead' in applauding my effort. Yet, having small jealousies trying to find doubt in my claim – "just saying - "unbelievable"!

Lois - Divorced me

Unhappy Ending: I never told my wife Lois: Of my involvement with Princess Diana until after It, and Diana was back in London. Because of Lois's feelings of hurt, maybe compromising the situation. But Lois seemed to somewhat overlooked it to some degree for business sake.

Lois and I still love each other. "But Lois can Not ever accept me being in Love with Diana, and us live together! "Yet, Lois knows - Hearts Change."

Darlin, Diana

Since Youv'e Gone

Nothin Last Forever !

Rich's

"Explanation Regarding"
Remarkable
Coincidences, Reincarnation, Paranormal, Phenomenal
and
Love at First Sight

I, Rich McDonough the author of this book, and a Private Detective was in fact married to Ethel McDonough and she passed away in 1982 at age 43. We had been together for some twenty six years, and I loved her dearly, then and now!

In the fall of 1993 I received a kidnapping assignment of an eleven year child, wrongfully taken by the bio-father after a domestic dispute. From the Kensington area of London England, United Kingdom.

The child was the life long endearing best childhood friend of Princess Diana of Wales, whom hired Rich to search, find and bring back the child to her friend.

From personal observations, notion, breath and passion of Ethel's transmigration soul, we believe may have passed to Princess Diana. And a definite past physical resemblance is prevalent.

GLOSSARY

"And now, basically for a better understanding of my quoted terms."

With this writer's Interpretation of the meanings in this book, you may be able to arrive at a somewhat logical feeling and be comfortable in your decision in what you
    Read in this book!

caption inscriptions - And Meanings.

Love at first Sight: An overwhelming sensation that
Feels like love – But isn't! (Per Webster's New World Thesaurus)

Basically: It's a good match of endorphins between two people, and in essence it's an indication of strong physical attraction, saying 'Love at first sight' can lead to lasting marriages, depending on one's thoughts and beliefs.

Coincidence: A, remarkable concurrence of events or circumstances that have no apparent causal connections with one another. The perception of such remarkable coincidence may lead to supernatural, and occult, or paranormal claims. 'They met by coincidence'

casual - connection - Not casual.
Unplanned or accidental - for coincidence.

The words above and their meanings are somewhat the foundation of parts of this story line. An understanding as to how they relate in the overall picture as to the importance of each, are crucial as to their belief and credibility. In this book

Coincidental: To me, and in my personal opinion relates to the unknown-unexplained and the supernatural. Which leaves a lot unanswered factors, all of which can and will be interpreted.

So, if you consider real known facts about a subject or person that you have known - to have been vibrant, energetic, vigorous, lively, active, attractive - Certainly to me has all the element components of a paranormal view, as in my case scenarios herein this book.

To me, each element of facts that enter into the basic story fundamentals in the initial stage basis, of thinking, or assuming 'one individual' in relating to another, could actually be your subject, as one in the same!

Again, to me - weighs out in the strength of realistic facts and or evidence reflecting strongly in some degree as proof, that's available. And even then, one can't be sure - "Live with it."

So, in my case herein, a good portion of the coincidental thoughts I'm basing parts of my book on, by treating one individual as two, in the book periodically in your opinion.

I'm trying to reflect to my readers, as to 'why' I have two named individuals in my book, inferring that they are one in the same.

It's your call. . . But realistically knowing they are TWO different persons, but being referred to and treated as one.

As well, considering 'Reincarnation' or little known as in Metempsychosis or Transmigration, of the Souls at death.

The soul then passes into another living creature, taking on their likeness and so on, reflecting almost total similarities.

And, if this is true then, real similar things, appearances, or acts you might recall of your subject should be reflected as well.

This book is being written as the 'second person' being the subject of the reincarnation event or book.

And the basic reasons as to why all the facts and information is incorporated as to the similarities between the two, such as.

The subject in question is very similar to another person who has passed, such as the ultimate likeness in looks, such as the face and physical attributes, peculiarity, characteristics, being so much like their subject – 'feeling the two are the same?'

Much of the similarities being close or the same as the Subjects

But are they?

No one will ever know-all you can do is assume and give the one with the likeness, the benefit of doubt – then move on with life, as you need!

The Princess Diana

We all knew Passed 25 years ago in 1997

Depending on your feelings and your decision, as to what you think is right. Along with what works for you, in this life time event!

"Will in-fact, be as life has meant it to be."

Glossary: Opinion of the author – Rich McDonough

Printed in the United States
by Baker & Taylor Publisher Services